Arkansas Bucket List Adventure Guide

Explore 100 Offbeat Destinations You Must Visit!

David Russell

Bridge Press
dp@purplelink.org

Please consider writing a review!
Just visit: purplelink.org/review

Copyright 2021. Bridge Press. All Rights Reserved.
No part of this book may be reproduced or transmitted in any form or by any means, electronic or mechanical, including photocopying, recording or by any other form without written permission from the publisher.

ISBN: 978-1-955149-41-9

FREE BONUS

Find Out 31 Incredible Places You Can Visit Next! Just Go to:

purplelink.org/travel

Table of Contents

How to Use This Book

Welcome to your very own adventure guide to exploring the many wonders of the state of Arkansas. Not only does this book layout the most wonderful places to visit and sights to see in the vast state, but it also provides driving directions and GPS coordinates for Google Maps to make exploring that much easier.

Adventure Guide

Sorted by region, this guide offers over 100 amazing wonders found in Arkansas for you to see and explore. These can be visited in any order, and this book will help you keep track of where you've been and where to look forward to going next. Each portion describes the area or place, what to look for, how to get there, and what you may need to bring along.

GPS Coordinates

As you can imagine, not all of the locations in this book have a physical address. Fortunately, some of our listed wonders are either located within a national park or reserve or are near a city, town, or place of business. For those that are not associated with a specific location, it is easiest to map it using GPS coordinates.

Luckily, Google has a system of codes that converts the coordinates into pin-drop locations that Google Maps is able to interpret and navigate.

Each adventure in this guide will include both the GPS coordinates and general directions on how to find the location.

It is important that you are prepared for poor cell signals. It's a good practice to route your location and ensure that the directions are accessible offline. Depending on your device and the distance of some locations, you may need to travel with a backup battery source.

About Arkansas

Arkansas's nickname is the Natural State, and once you visit, you'll understand why. Its landscape is full of natural wonders, including mountains, lakes, streams, valleys, farms, and plains. Arkansas is the smallest state west of the Mississippi, but that doesn't mean you can't have big adventures there, especially given the diverse landscape and multitude of outdoor activities available to explore.

The state was formed as part of the Louisiana Purchase in 1803 and became a separate territory 16 years later in 1819. Little Rock was named the capital of the state in 1820. In 1836, Arkansas gained statehood, becoming the 25th state admitted to the Union. More than 19 million acres of Arkansas are covered in forests, comprising over half of the state and providing significant resources to the rest of the country. In addition to timber, Arkansas is a primary source of bromine, petroleum, silica sandstone, and natural gas. Other key industries in the state include aerospace and defense, paper, and food and beverage.

The only currently active diamond mind in the United States is in Arkansas, which makes it a high-priority tourist attraction for visitors to the state. However, there are plenty of other fantastic places to see and things to do for visitors of all ages, including fishing, hiking, spelunking, hunting, swimming, boating, and more. You'll never lack outdoor fun in Arkansas! And if you're into American history, you'll discover plenty of historical landmarks here as well, including Little Rock Central High School, which became the first integrated school in the country following the groundbreaking Supreme Court case of *Brown v. the Board of Education of Topeka.*

Whether you're looking to connect with nature or with America's past, Arkansas has got you covered. This little state is packed with opportunities for entertainment, education, and leisure. Once you visit, you may never want to leave. At the very least, you'll have to plan another trip to see everything Arkansas has to offer.

Landscape and Climate

You'll find a little bit of every climate in Arkansas because of its location and range of elevations. It's mostly considered a humid, subtropical state, which means its summers are hot and its winters are cool. However, you may find snow atop its highest mountain in December and January, so be prepared for any weather conditions when you visit.

At the peak of summer in July, Arkansas has an average high temperature of 93°F, but the humidity can make it seem significantly warmer. In the southern part of the state, temperatures routinely exceed 100°F and can get as high as 110°. Winters at the lower elevations are generally mild, with an average high temperature of 51°F in January. The low temperature rarely drops below 32°F, but occasionally you may see snow at higher elevations.

The state is essentially divided into two landscapes, with the mountainous region to the north and the lowlands to the south. It borders Missouri to the north, Tennessee and Mississippi to the east, Louisiana to the south, and Oklahoma and Texas to the west and southwest. It shares the Ozark Mountains with Missouri, which offer some of the most gorgeous views in all of America.

The spring and fall are ideal seasons for visiting any of the state's five regions, as they all experience mild temperatures and generally sunny days during these months. Expect the northern part of the state to become colder earlier in the year, but even then, it's still usually temperate enough to visit year-round. You may encounter thunderstorms and flooding between March and May, but severe weather is typically short-lived, even during spring, which is the most volatile season for storms in Arkansas.

Tanyard Creek Nature Trail

Below the Windsor Lake Dam in Bella Vista, you'll find the Tanyard Creek Nature Trail, an off-the-beaten-path trail that winds through northwest Arkansas. As you hike this well-marked loop, you'll be treated to a second-growth oak and hickory forest, a gorgeous waterfall, and rumbling rapids. You can fish in the deeper parts of the creek, with smallmouth bass, largemouth bass, and carp of all sizes just waiting to be caught. Even though there are several bridges along the trail, many hikers bypass them by crossing the creek using rock stepping stones. Just be careful because they might be slippery if the creek is running high.

Best Time to Visit: The only time that's not good to visit the Tanyard Creek Nature Trail is during the winter.

Pass/Permit/Fees: There is no fee to visit the Tanyard Creek Nature Trail, but you will need a fishing license if you decide to fish.

Closest City or Town: Bella Vista

How to Get There: From Bella Vista: Take Cooper Road east toward Hatcher Drive. Turn right onto W. Lancashire Boulevard. Go a half-mile, then turn left onto Nature Trail Lane. From there, it's 350 feet to the trailhead.

GPS Coordinates: 36.4719° N, -94.2610° W

Did You Know? Tanyard Creek Nature Trail was constructed by volunteers and has two paths. One is a paved walking trail, and the other is a well-maintained natural surface trail.

Crystal Bridges Museum of American Art

Named for a natural spring located near the facility and for the bridge design incorporated into the structure, the Crystal Bridges Museum of American Art is a work of art in and of itself. World-renowned architect Moshe Safdie designed a series of pavilions for galleries, classrooms, meeting spaces, and a glass-enclosed gathering hall around two picturesque spring-fed ponds to create a museum that integrates seamlessly into its natural surroundings. In addition to the American artwork displayed inside the museum, you'll also discover a library with over 50,000 volumes of art reference books, five miles of walking trails surrounded by sculptures, a restaurant, a coffee shop, and a museum store.

Best Time to Visit: The museum is open from 10:00 a.m. to 6:00 p.m., Saturday through Monday, and from 10:00 a.m. to 9:00 p.m., Wednesday through Friday.

Pass/Permit/Fees: There is no fee to visit the Crystal Bridges Museum of American Art.

Closest City or Town: Bentonville

How to Get There: From Little Rock: Take I-40 West for 214 miles to E. Central Avenue in Bentonville. Take Exit 88B, and travel for 1.9 miles on NE John Deshields Boulevard to Museum Way, where the museum is located.

GPS Coordinates: 36.3834° N, -94.2027° W

Did You Know? The permanent collection at the museum includes American artwork from five centuries, including pieces made by indigenous people and early settlers.

Museum of Native American History

Originally named the Museum of Native American Artifacts when it was opened in 2006, the collection quickly grew, and the museum needed a new name and space to better reflect the organization's purpose. It was renamed the Museum of Native American History, or MONAH, in 2008. The museum is home to more than 10,000 Native American artifacts, many of which came from the personal collection of David Bogle, the founder and a registered member of the Cherokee Nation. Visitors to the museum will travel through 14,000 years of Native American history spanning five time periods. Additionally, temporary exhibits that showcase a specific time period or tribe are featured at the museum on an annual basis.

Best Time to Visit: The museum is open to timed visits from 10:00 a.m. to 3:00 p.m., Tuesday through Saturday.

Pass/Permit/Fees: There is no fee to visit the Museum of Native American History.

Closest City or Town: Bentonville

How to Get There: From the north or south: Take Exit 88 B onto E. Central Avenue. Drive past the square and cross Walton Boulevard. You will see the museum on your left on O Street.

GPS Coordinates: 36.3721° N, -94.2310° W

Did You Know? Some of the incredible artifacts you'll see at the MONAH include a Sioux quilled pipe bag, a Jama-Coaque ceramic effigy, and a Nasca vase.

The Walmart Museum

This museum documents the rise of Walmart, one of the largest companies and employers in the nation. It opened in 1990 as the Walmart Visitor Center but eventually was renamed The Walmart Museum to better reflect its purpose. By touring the exhibits and viewing the artifacts present in this museum, you'll discover the story of Sam Walton and his growth as a leader and businessman. Several long-time Walmart associates were involved in the museum's creation, gathering artifacts and stories to tell the tale of Walmart's legacy.

Best Time to Visit: The Walmart Museum is open from 10:00 a.m. to 8:00 p.m. every day of the week. Since it's indoors, it's a good attraction to visit any time of the year.

Pass/Permit/Fees: There is no fee to visit The Walmart Museum.

Closest City or Town: Bentonville

How to Get There: From Little Rock: Take I-40 West for 212 miles to 8th Street in Bentonville. Take Exit 87 onto 8th Street. Drive for 2.4 miles to E. Central Avenue, where the museum is located.

GPS Coordinates: 36.3731° N, -94.2092° W

Did You Know? The museum features information about the Walton 5&10, the first store to bear the Walton name. It was a Ben Franklin five-and-dime store, located next door to a barber shop, a space that Walton eventually acquired to expand his 5&10 shop and turn his small business into a major success story.

Cosmic Cavern

Located between Eureka Springs and Branson, Missouri, Cosmic Cavern is the largest privately owned cave in Arkansas. It was discovered in 1845 but didn't open to public viewing until 1927. It stays at a constant 64°F all year long. On the 1-hour-and-15-minute tour, you'll be treated to a nine-foot soda straw structure and two bottomless lakes, including "Silent Splendor," which was just discovered in 1993.

Best Time to Visit: Since the cave stays at a consistent temperature all year, it's a warm place to visit in the winter and a cool place to visit in the summer.

Pass/Permit/Fees: Adult admission is $20, and children between the ages of 5 and 12 are $10.

Closest City or Town: Berryville

How to Get There: From Little Rock: Take I-40 West to Arkansas 103/N. Springfield Avenue in Green Forest. Follow this road for 161 miles to Arkansas 21 South. Follow Arkansas 21 South for 13.4 miles to the cave's entrance.

From Branson, Missouri: Take US-65 Business South to Arkansas 21 South. Continue for 27.6 miles to the cave's entrance.

GPS Coordinates: 36.4354° N, -93.4990° W

Did You Know? Cosmic Cavern was discovered when John Moore and his two sons were in the Ozarks prospecting for lead.

Bull Shoals Caverns

Located in northern Arkansas, Bull Shoals Caverns is one of the oldest limestone cavern systems in the world and certainly the oldest in the Ozarks. In the deepest part of the cave, you'll discover a waterfall that is partially responsible for the caverns' development. While the caverns were opened to tourism in 1958, carbon dating indicates that Native Americans lived in the caves approximately 10,000 years earlier.

Best Time to Visit: The caverns are open between March 15 and October 31. The best time to visit during their open season is in the summer when the cool 59°F tour will provide relief from the heat and humidity.

Pass/Permit/Fees: Adult admission is $19.95, and children between the ages of 5 and 11 cost $9.95 each.

Closest City or Town: Bull Shoals

How to Get There: From Little Rock: Take I-40 West to Arkansas 27 in Marshall. Take Arkansas 17 North to Arkansas 14 West. After 34 miles, turn right on US-412 East/US-62 East in Yellville. Follow the road for 5 miles to AR-178 East. Take AR-178 East to C S Woods Boulevard in Bull Shoals to Bull Shoals Caverns.

GPS Coordinates: 36.3794° N, -92.5842° W

Did You Know? Bull Shoals Caverns formed about 350 million years ago. They are home to nearly every known type of cave formation found in the U.S., including stalagmites, stalactites, columns, flow stone, and cave pearls, among others.

White River

This 720-mile river begins at Bull Shoals Lake, wanders up through southern Missouri, and comes back into Arkansas near Cotter. Its flow is interrupted by six dams in Arkansas and two in Missouri. A relatively calm river, it does get rough during the spring's rainy season. The upper river is a paradise for anglers, with a variety of bass, catfish, and sunfish available to catch. Flyfishing and trout fishing are popular below Bull Shoals Dam. White River State Park is on the shores of both the White River and Bull Shoals Lake. It features boating, hiking, and mountain biking opportunities.

Best Time to Visit: Fishing is best in the spring, right after it's stocked with trout.

Pass/Permit/Fees: There is no fee to visit the White River, but there are guided fishing trips available at various rates.

Closest City or Town: Bull Shoals

How to Get There: From Little Rock: Take I-40 West to Arkansas 27 North in Marshall. Go 97.1 miles to Arkansas 14. Travel west on Arkansas 14 for 34.2 miles to US-412 East/US-62 East in Yellville. Turn right onto US-412 E/US-62 East. Travel this road for 4.8 miles, then take Arkansas 178 East. Drive to Powerhouse Road to reach the park's entrance.

GPS Coordinates: 33.8834° N, -91.0690° W

Did You Know? The White River is a major Mississippi River tributary that was frequented by steamboats in the mid-1800s.

DeGray Lake Resort State Park

First-class accommodations, a variety of activities, and scenic views of DeGray Lake are just some of the features of DeGray Lake Resort Park. No matter what you're into, there's sure to be something for you to do here. From an 18-hole championship golf course to Rent-A-Yurts, you'll never have a boring moment at this state park. Of course, you can also find plenty of hiking, mountain biking, and horseback riding trails in and around the park, but you won't be restricted to just those activities. Don't forget to have a meal or two at the Shoreline Restaurant, which offers delectable dishes for breakfast, lunch, and dinner.

Best Time to Visit: Early fall and winter are the best times to visit DeGray Lake Resort State Park because the temperatures will be more moderate, allowing you to participate in all the outdoor activities available to guests.

Pass/Permit/Fees: There is no fee to visit DeGray Lake Resort State Park unless you stay overnight.

Closest City or Town: Bismarck

How to Get There: From Little Rock: Take I-30 West for 63.4 miles to Arkansas 7/Valley Street in Caddo Valley. Take Exit 78 onto Arkansas 7. Drive for 8.7 miles to State Park Entrance Road.

GPS Coordinates: 34.2457° N, -93.1481° W

Did You Know? DeGray Lake Resort State Park is the only resort state park in Arkansas. It has been in operation since 1972.

Natural Bridge of Arkansas

The Natural Bridge of Arkansas is a 100-foot sandstone formation that was used as a bridge during the days of the first settlers. Currently, visitors are not able to walk or drive across the bridge in order to preserve its natural structure. However, it is the perfect backdrop for photos, and there is a log cabin and moonshiner's still that can be explored on site. You'll enjoy the artifacts collected and displayed by this private owner and get an extensive history lesson as well.

Best Time to Visit: With all the flowers on the property, spring makes it the most colorful time to visit. Fall is gorgeous, too, with the vibrant colors of the changing leaves. It only operates between March and October.

Pass/Permit/Fees: Admission is $5.00 per person.

Closest City or Town: Clinton

How to Get There: From the South: Take US-65 North for about 3.5 miles to where it splits from Highway 9 in Clinton. Head east on Natural Bridge Road, then drive one mile to the entrance.

From the North: Take Highway 65 to Natural Bridge Road, which is 15.5 miles south of Highway 66 in Leslie. Take Natural Bridge Road east for one mile to the entrance.

GPS Coordinates: 35.6561° N, -92.4484° W

Did You Know? The Quapaw Indians once settled in the area of Clinton and used the stone bridge to cross Little Johnny Creek.

Hemmed-in-Hollow Falls

This 209-foot waterfall is the tallest waterfall located between the Appalachians and the Rocky Mountains. The geological canyon surrounding the waterfall is simply incredible and will make you feel tiny as you look up to the top of the falls. The hike to the falls is challenging and not recommended for small children or people who have difficulty walking. It's not far (just 2.5 miles each way), but it's steep and rocky.

Best Time to Visit: Hemmed-in-Hollow Falls is spectacular during a rainstorm, so spring and early summer are ideal times to visit. Be sure to get to the falls by 9:30 a.m. to get the best photographs.

Pass/Permit/Fees: There is no fee to visit the Hemmed-in-Hollow Falls.

Closest City or Town: Compton

How to Get There: From Ponca: Take Highway 43 North for 9 miles to reach Compton. There will be a gravel road to your right that is marked with a "Wilderness Access" sign. A vacant store will be across from the road. Turn onto the gravel road, and take a right about a block later. Drive another mile until you see a sign marking the Hemmed-in-Hollow trailhead on the left.

GPS Coordinates: 36.0721° N, -93.3074° W

Did You Know? If you visit the Hemmed-in-Hollow Falls during a dry period, there will be no waterfall at all, so be mindful of recent precipitation before attempting the challenging hike only to find that the falls aren't flowing.

Cadron Settlement Park

This 150-acre park located in Conway is leased from the U.S. Army Corps of Engineers. It's a designated national historical site due to its roots as a French trading post. Amenities at the park include a boat launching ramp, restrooms, picnic areas, and plenty of parking. Be sure to see the Blockhouse restoration at the park and take note that the Cherokee Trail of Tears passes through the area. There are several hiking trails through the park, many of which are handicap accessible. The park gets its name from the first permanent white settlement near the Arkansas River, approximately 5 miles west of Conway. At the time, in the early 1800s, approximately 40 white families lived in the vicinity of Cadron Creek.

Best Time to Visit: The park is open year-round but is best visited during the warmer months of the year, especially for water activities.

Pass/Permit/Fees: There is no fee to visit Cadron Settlement Park unless you want to reserve a pavilion.

Closest City or Town: Conway

How to Get There: From Little Rock: Take I-40 West for 36.3 miles to Arkansas State Highway 25 South/Salem Road in Conway. Take Exit 124B onto US-64, then drive for 5.4 miles to the park's entrance.

GPS Coordinates: 35.1078° N, -92.5449° W

Did You Know? Before this area was a park, it served as a stopping place for the Butterfield Overland Mail Route.

Jack's Ultra Sports Paintball & Laser Tag

For an afternoon filled with activity, visit Jack's Ultra Sports Paintball & Laser Tag, where you'll find low-impact paintball matches, laser tag games, escape rooms, archery games, and an arcade with prizes. Kids and adults of all ages will love these indoor activities, especially when they can't get outside because of the weather. Packages are available so that you can enjoy several activities at one low price. The facility is excellent for parties and group teambuilding events, but you'll find something fun to do even if you visit by yourself.

Best Time to Visit: This fun center is open on Friday from 5:00 p.m. to 9:00 p.m., Saturday from 1:00 p.m. to 9:00 p.m., and Sunday from 1:00 p.m. to 6:00 p.m.

Pass/Permit/Fees: Fees to visit Jack's Ultra Sports Paintball & Laser Tag vary based on the activities you choose. They start at $24.99 per player for a paintball game.

Closest City or Town: Conway

How to Get There: From Little Rock: Take I-40 West for 29.6 miles to US-65 North/E. Dave Ward Drive in Conway. Take Exit 129A-B and drive for 0.7 miles to Equity Avenue, where the center is located.

GPS Coordinates: 35.0707° N, -92.4247° W

Did You Know? You can bundle multiple activities to get a better price. For example, you can have two paintball games and one laser tag game for $34.98 instead of $24.99 for two paintball games alone.

Thunder Alley Grand Prix

Go-karts and arcade games await adventurous visitors to the Thunder Alley Grand Prix. Driving go-karts on the best track in town is the highlight of this attraction, and you can zoom along the road in a single kart or grab a friend and ride together in a double-seat kart. When you need a break from the race, get some tokens and hit the arcade. You'll find games like skeeball, air hockey, and Dance Dance Revolution, all of which will dispense prize tickets as your score climbs higher and higher.

Best Time to Visit: Thunder Alley Grand Prix is open Monday through Thursday from 11:00 a.m. to 10:00 p.m., Friday and Saturday from 11:00 a.m. to 11:00 p.m., and Sunday from 12:00 p.m. to 10:00 p.m. The go-kart track is outdoors, so this is best visited in the warmer months, but the games can be comfortably enjoyed any time of the year.

Pass/Permit/Fees: A single go-kart ride is $6, and a double-seat kart is $7. You can also purchase four rides in a single kart for $18 or four rides in a double kart for $21.

Closest City or Town: Conway

How to Get There: From Little Rock: Take I-40 West for 29.6 miles to US-65 North. Take the exit onto US-65 North, and drive 4.7 miles to Dave Ward Road, where the facility is located.

GPS Coordinates: 35.0713° N, -92.4949° W

Did You Know? You can get a single go-kart ride for ten guests for $100, two rides for ten guests for $150, or three rides for ten guests for $200, along with other benefits.

Mount Nebo

Mount Nebo State Park is located at the top of the 1,350-foot Mount Nebo, making it one of the highest parks in the state. In fact, RVs over 24 feet in length are not allowed up the 18%-grade Highway 155 West that leads to the park since it's extremely narrow and has 11 switchbacks. The sweeping views from the top of the mountain will take your breath away. There are 14 cabins with bluff views and 35 campsites in the park that allow you to wake up to spectacular sunrises before beginning your wonder-filled day.

Best Time to Visit: Spring and fall are the ideal times to visit because of the wildflowers and the color-changing leaves.

Pass/Permit/Fees: There is no fee to visit Mount Nebo State Park, but there are fees to stay overnight in the cabins or campgrounds.

Closest City or Town: Dardanelle

How to Get There: From Little Rock: Take I-40 West to Arkansas 363 South in Pottsville. At Exit 88, take Arkansas 247 North to State Highway 155. Continue 14.2 miles through Yell County to the park's entrance.

GPS Coordinates: 35.2174° N, -93.2467° W

Did You Know? Mount Nebo State Park is the second-oldest state park in Arkansas. It spans more than 3,000 acres. Mount Nebo was a major landmark for travelers on the Arkansas River in the 19th and 20th centuries.

Onyx Cave

The Onyx Cave is the oldest show cave in Arkansas, having hosted visitors since 1893, just two years after its discovery. The 30-minute self-guided tour of this smallish cave is suitable for all ages, although no strollers are allowed in the cave itself. Enjoy various chambers throughout the cave, including the Friendly Dragon and the Witches' Fireplace

Best Time to Visit: Since the cave is always a cool 57°F no matter what time of year you visit, this is one attraction that can be planned year-round. It will cool you down during hot summers and will require only a jacket in the winter. The cave is open from 9:00 a.m. to 4:00 p.m. in the winter and from 9:00 a.m. to 5:00 p.m. in the summer.

Pass/Permit/Fees: Adult admission is $10.00; children between the ages of 3 and 12 are $6.00.

Closest City or Town: Eureka Springs

How to Get There: From downtown Eureka Springs, take Onyx Cave Lane for 6 miles, following the signs along the way. The 15-minute drive will take you through the gorgeous Ozarks Mountains to the cave's visitor center. There will be an intermediate hike from the parking area to the visitor center.

GPS Coordinates: 36.4420° N, -93.6824° W

Did You Know? The Onyx Cave was the setting for the cave scenes in the 1969 science fiction film: *It's Alive!*

Ozark Mountains

The Ozark Mountains are made up of three distinct plateaus: Boston, Salem, and Springfield. They span approximately 1.2 million acres across Arkansas, Missouri, Oklahoma, Kansas, and Illinois. The 165-mile Ozarks Highlands Trail will take you from Lake Fort Smith State Park to the Buffalo National River. It is one of the longest hiking trails in the United States. Camping, rock climbing, fishing, floating, and mountain biking are just some of the activities you can participate in when visiting the Ozark Mountains.

Best Time to Visit: The spring is the best time to visit the Ozarks.

Pass/Permit/Fees: In the Arkansas part of the Ozarks, there is no fee to visit unless you're staying overnight. Camping fees vary based on the campground you visit, so call ahead for pricing.

Closest City or Town: Fayetteville, Bentonville, Clarksville, Springdale, Eureka Springs, and Fort Smith

How to Get There: From Clarksville, take Arkansas Highway 64 to Arkansas Highway 21, then continue to the Buffalo National River.

GPS Coordinates: 36.5693° N, -93.0977° W

Did You Know? The Ozarks are the largest mountains between the Appalachians in the east and the Rocky Mountains in the west. Many of these mountains exceed 2,000 feet.

Thorncrown Chapel

A spiritual experience in a woodland setting awaits you at the 48-foot Thorncrown Chapel in the Ozark Mountains. This incredible wooden structure opened in 1980 and contains more than 6,000 square feet of glass, making up 425 windows. Thorncrown Chapel is often referred to as "one of the finest religious spaces of modern times" and has won several architectural awards. This is a functional church that has Sunday services at 9:00 a.m. and 11:00 a.m. from April through October and 11:00 a.m. in November and December. It is not open during January and February.

Best Time to Visit: You can visit the chapel between 9:00 a.m. and 5:00 p.m. between April and November. In December and March, you can visit between 11:00 a.m. and 4:00 p.m.

Pass/Permit/Fees: There is no fee to visit Thorncrown Chapel.

Closest City or Town: Eureka Springs

How to Get There: From Eureka Springs: Take S. Main Street southwest toward Benton Street. Turn right on Benton Street, then right again on Midway Street. Continue onto US-62 West/W. Van Buren and travel for 2.4 miles to the chapel.

GPS Coordinates: 36.4184° N, -93.7716° W

Did You Know? Architect E. Fay Jones designed the Thorncrown Chapel. His inspiration was Sainte Chappelle in Paris, a light-filled Gothic church that led Jones to call the Thorncrown Chapel's style "Ozark Gothic."

Baum-Walker Stadium

Originally called Baum Stadium at George Cole Field, the stadium was renamed the Baum-Walker Stadium at George Cole Field in 2015 to recognize the contributions of longtime supporters Willard and Pat Walker, as well as the Walker Family. The stadium is considered one of the best college baseball fields in the U.S., and officials from other universities across the country have sought blueprints and tours to replicate the facility at their own schools. It has the capacity for 10,737 fans but broke a single-game attendance record against Auburn in 2014 when 11,742 visitors filled the stands. It was built in 1996, and the first game was played on April 13 of that year against Auburn.

Best Time to Visit: The best time to visit Baum-Walker Stadium is during baseball season, which occurs in spring, summer, and early fall.

Pass/Permit/Fees: The cost to visit Baum-Walker Stadium varies based on game and seat selection.

Closest City or Town: Fayetteville

How to Get There: From Little Rock: Take I-40 West for 188 miles to Arkansas State Highway 112 North/S. Cato Springs Road in Fayetteville. Take Exit 60 onto Arkansas 112, then drive for 1.2 miles to the stadium.

GPS Coordinates: 36.0505° N, -94.18224° W

Did You Know? The field at Baum-Walker Stadium is named for former Arkansas athletic director George Cole, who was also a football coach at the University of Arkansas for 25 years.

Botanical Gardens of the Ozarks

You won't find another botanical garden like this one located in the Ozark mountains. Its grassroots beginnings, built solely by volunteers, give it a whimsical feel that is entirely approachable and enjoyable. The concept for these botanical gardens was to create a circle of "themed backyard gardens" designed to teach local citizens about gardening in northwest Arkansas. The region has a challenging environment in which many plants struggle to survive. Currently, there are 12 backyard gardens on the site, along with the Totemeier Horticulture Center, which houses the only butterfly house in Arkansas.

Best Time to Visit: The Botanical Gardens of the Ozarks are open from 9:00 a.m. to 5:00 p.m., Friday through Wednesday, and are closed on Thursday. The best time to visit is during the spring and early summer when the gardens are in bloom.

Pass/Permit/Fees: Adult admission is $10.00. Children between the ages of 4 and 12 are $5.00. Children ages three and under are free.

Closest City or Town: Fayetteville

How to Get There: From Little Rock: Take I-40 West for 196 miles to US-71 North in Fayetteville. Take E. Joyce Boulevard for 3.1 miles to the gardens' entrance.

GPS Coordinates: 36.1363° N, -94.1185° W

Did You Know? More than 70,000 people visit the Botanical Gardens of the Ozarks each year.

Bud Walton Arena Hall of Champions Museum

On the ground level of the Bud Walton Arena, you'll find the Hall of Champions Museum, which features the history of the University of Arkansas athletics. The Bud Walton Arena is named for James "Bud" Walton. He donated at least $15 million to fund the construction of the arena and the museum. The arena is home to the University of Arkansas basketball teams and has a seating capacity of 19,368.

Best Time to Visit: The museum is open Monday through Friday from 8:00 a.m. to 5:00 p.m. and when there is a basketball game. The best time to visit if you want to avoid crowds is during the off-season for basketball.

Pass/Permit/Fees: There is no fee to visit the Bud Walton Arena Hall of Champions Museum.

Closest City or Town: Fayetteville

How to Get There: From Little Rock: Take I-40 West for 188 miles to Arkansas State Highway 112 North/S. Cato Springs Road in Fayetteville. Take Exit 60 onto Arkansas 112, and follow for 2 miles to Nolan Richardson Drive.

GPS Coordinates: 36.0618° N, -94.1782° W

Did You Know? You'll discover even the most obscure history about campus events at this museum, including the appearance of Howdy Doody and Buffalo Bob in the 1970s.

Donald W. Reynolds Razorback Stadium

Serving as the home field for the University of Arkansas Razorbacks football team, Donald W. Reynolds Razorback Stadium is a 76,000-seat facility that originally opened in 1941 as Razorback Stadium. In 2001, the stadium was renamed to honor Donald W. Reynolds, whose foundation donated $21 million in 1999 to assist with the renovation of the stadium. The field at the stadium is named for the school's former athletic director Frank Broyles, who was instrumental in getting the $65 million stadium renovation and expansion passed in 1998.

Best Time to Visit: The best time to visit Donald W. Reynolds Razorback Stadium is during football season, which is in the fall and early winter.

Pass/Permit/Fees: The cost to visit Donald W. Reynolds Razorback Stadium is dependent on seat and event selection.

Closest City or Town: Fayetteville

How to Get There: From Little Rock: Take I-40 West for 186 miles to Arkansas State Highway 112 North/S. Cato Springs Road in Fayetteville. Take Exit 60 onto Arkansas 112, and follow the signs to Razorback Road for 2.3 miles to reach the stadium.

GPS Coordinates: 36.0688° N, -94.1788° W

Did You Know? In 2000, the Donald W. Reynolds Razorback Stadium boasted the largest LED screen in a sports arena at 30 by 107 feet in size.

Fayetteville Downtown Square & Gardens

Spend a day visiting quaint shops, eating at unique restaurants, exploring historic buildings, and enjoying vibrant flowers in Fayetteville Downtown Square & Gardens. The Downtown Square has been a public park and plaza since 1978. One of the most popular events held in the square and gardens is the Lights of the Ozarks Festival, which occurs every December. Additionally, there is a farmers market in the square every Tuesday, Thursday, and Saturday between April and November.

Best Time to Visit: December is the best time to visit the Fayetteville Downtown Square & Gardens if you want the full holiday experience. The gardens are carefully tended all year but are best visited in the spring and early summer.

Pass/Permit/Fees: There is no fee to visit the Fayetteville Downtown Square & Gardens.

Closest City or Town: Fayetteville

How to Get There: From Little Rock: Take I-40 West for 186 miles to Arkansas State Highway 112 North/S. Cato Springs Road in Fayetteville. Take Exit 60 onto Arkansas 112, then travel for 3.4 miles to W. Center Street, where the square and gardens are located.

GPS Coordinates: 36.0629° N, -94.1604° W

Did You Know? In addition to the Old Post Office, other historic buildings in the square include the Old Bank of Fayetteville Building and the Mrs. Young Building.

Lake Fayetteville

Anglers flock to Lake Fayetteville's 194 acres of water, where they can catch a variety of fish, including catfish, red ear, carp, goggle-eye, blue gill, crappie, and bass. Fishing gear and a boat can be rented from the on-site marina, or you're welcome to fish from the shore. There is a 5.5-mile hiking trail around the lake or a 4.3-mile hard-surface multi-use trail designed for cyclists, skaters, and other non-motorized vehicles. Bicycles can also be rented in the park. A disc golf course is available, but you'll need to bring your own equipment for that activity.

Best Time to Visit: The marina closes between December 23 and January 15. It is best to visit during the summer to take full advantage of all of the activities available.

Pass/Permit/Fees: There is no fee to visit Lake Fayetteville unless you want to rent equipment.

Closest City or Town: Fayetteville

How to Get There: From Little Rock: Take I-40 West for 194 miles to US-71 North in Fayetteville. Drive for 1.5 miles on US-71 to reach the park's entrance.

GPS Coordinates: 36.1412° N, -94.1293° W

Did You Know? Lake Fayetteville was created in 1949 as a source of drinking water for Fayetteville and the surrounding area. However, ten years later, the Beaver Water District was created to provide the area with water from Beaver Lake. Lake Fayetteville was designated for recreational use.

TheatreSquared

Over 55,000 visitors come to TheatreSquared each year to attend locally produced productions. Trained artists from all over the United States produce approximately 320 performances each year, including those presented in the theatre, in schools, and online. Several professional playwrights continuously develop scripts through the Arkansas New Play Festival. Winner of the 2020 American Architecture Award, the 50,000-square-foot property includes two intimate theatres, artists' apartments, rehearsal space, three-level commons, and outdoor gathering spaces.

Best Time to Visit: There are shows available all year round, so the best time to visit is when your desired show is on stage.

Pass/Permit/Fees: The cost to attend a show at TheatreSquared varies based on the production and seating choices.

Closest City or Town: Fayetteville

How to Get There: From Little Rock: Take I-40 West for 186 miles to Arkansas Highway 112 North/S. Cato Springs Road in Fayetteville. Take Exit 60 onto Arkansas 112 North, then drive for 3.2 miles to W. Spring Street, where the theatre is located.

GPS Coordinates: 36.0653° N, -94.1653° W

Did You Know? TheatreSquared has received critical acclaim on a national level, making *The New York Times* "Best Theater of 2020" list.

The Arkansas Air & Military Museum

This museum, established in 1986, is designed to display aircraft, artifacts related to aviation, and military memorabilia with specific attention to objects related to Arkansas. In the museum's permanent collection, you'll find restorations of historic aircraft, such as the Boeing-Stearman PT-17 N2S-S, the A-7B Corsair II, and a Westinghouse J34-WE-48 turbojet. Several ground vehicles and artifacts are on exhibit as well.

Best Time to Visit: The Arkansas Air & Military Museum is open Tuesday through Saturday from 11:00 a.m. to 4:00 p.m. It is closed on Sunday and Monday. There are various events held at the museum, which are often outside. For these events, summer is the best time to visit the museum.

Pass/Permit/Fees: Adult admission is $10. Children between the ages of 6 and 16 are $5. Children ages five and under and veterans are free.

Closest City or Town: Fayetteville

How to Get There: From Little Rock: Take I-40 West for 184 miles to N. Wilson Street in Greenland. Take Exit 58 onto W. Wilson Street, and drive for 2.1 miles to US-71 North/N. Main Avenue in Fayetteville, where the museum is located.

GPS Coordinates: 36.0080° N, -94.1731° W

Did You Know? Various temporary exhibits come through the museum and can be viewed at no additional cost, including *Decorations of a Different Kind* and *The Forgotten Wars*.

The Clinton House Museum

The Clinton House Museum documented the lives of former president Bill Clinton and former secretary of state Hillary Rodham Clinton when they lived in Fayetteville. The collections serve to showcase the Clintons' participation in their community as civic leaders and demonstrate their commitment to public service. The one-bedroom, 1,800-square-foot house was the Clintons' first home, nearly 20 years before they would move into the White House. The Tudor-revival-style home was built in 1931 and is located in the scenic Ozark Mountains.

Best Time to Visit: It is recommended to check the Museum's website for temporary closures before visiting. The First Ladies Garden behind the house is always open to the public and is best viewed in spring and early summer.

Pass/Permit/Fees: There is no fee to visit the Clinton House Museum or the First Ladies Garden, but donations are appreciated.

Closest City or Town: Fayetteville

How to Get There: From Little Rock: Take I-40 West for 188 miles to Arkansas State Highway 112 North/S. Cato Springs Road in Fayetteville. Take Exit 60 and drive for 2.4 miles to W. Clinton Drive, where the house is located.

GPS Coordinates: 36.0639° N, -94.1739° W

Did You Know? The Clintons left Fayetteville in 1976 but continued to rent the house to college students before selling it in 1983.

The Fayetteville Farmers Market

Founded in 1973, the Fayetteville Farmers Market has been committed to providing a selection of fresh, locally grown produce and goods to residents in northwest Arkansas. The market is open year-round. In addition to the freshest produce in the state, you'll also find meat, honey, baked goods, eggs, jams, and fine arts and crafts from producers who make or grow their products within 60 miles of Fayetteville. The market is proud to be the only certified Arkansas Grown and Arkansas Made location of its kind, as 100% of the items you'll find there are local products.

Best Time to Visit: The market is open all year long on Tuesday, Thursday, and Saturday from 7:00 a.m. to 1:00 p.m. The best time to visit is when your favorite fruit or vegetable is in season.

Pass/Permit/Fees: There is no fee to visit the Fayetteville Farmers Market, but be sure to bring money if you plan to buy any of the incredible products for sale there.

Closest City or Town: Fayetteville

How to Get There: From Little Rock: Take I-40 West for 188 miles to Arkansas State Highway 112 North/S. Cato Springs Road in Fayetteville. Take Exit 60 onto Arkansas 112, and drive for 3.4 miles to W. Center Street, where the market is located.

GPS Coordinates: 36.0633° N, -94.1606° W

Did You Know? Approximately 60 vendors set up shop at the Fayetteville Farmers Market three days a week.

The Walton Arts Center

In the 1980s, the University of Arkansas, the City of Fayetteville, and the Walton family joined together to conceive of a venue that could showcase local and regional performing arts productions, as well as major touring acts. The result was the 1,200-seat Walton Arts Center, which was completed in April 1992. Currently, the Walton Arts Center presents the most performing arts productions in the state, bringing entertainers and artists to the region from all over the world.

Best Time to Visit: There are shows at the Walton Arts Center year-round.

Pass/Permit/Fees: The cost to attend a show at the Walton Arts Center will vary based on the production and seat selections.

Closest City or Town:
Fayetteville

How to Get There: From Little Rock: Take I-40 West for 186 miles to Arkansas Highway 112 North/S. Cato Springs Road in Fayetteville. Take Exit 60 onto Arkansas 112 North, then drive for 3.3 miles to W. Dickson Street, where the center is located.

GPS Coordinates: 36.0672° N, -94.1647° W

Did You Know? After its initial construction, the Walton Arts Center underwent a $23 million renovation and expansion to add more event and production support space. More than 30,000 square feet were added.

Wilson Park

Wilson Park is the oldest park in Fayetteville. It encompasses 22.75 acres in the center of the city. Features that draw visitors to Wilson Park include the municipal Wilson Park Pool, a spring-fed pond, gorgeous gardens, and even a "castle," which is actually an art installation created by Frank Williams, a local artist. The castle and the picturesque backdrop of the park make this spot one of the most photographed areas in Fayetteville. Before the pool was built, the spring-fed into "Trent's Pond."

Best Time to Visit: The best time to visit the swimming pool is between Memorial Day and Labor Day since it closes after that date. The remainder of the park is open year-round.

Pass/Permit/Fees: There is no fee to visit Wilson Park, but to swim in the pool, adults are $4, and children are $3.

Closest City or Town: Fayetteville

How to Get There: From Little Rock: Take I-40 West for 190 miles to W. Wedington Drive in Fayetteville. Take Exit 64, then drive for 2.4 miles to N. Park Avenue, where the park is located.

GPS Coordinates: 36.0729° N, -94.1615° W

Did You Know? In the 1970s, the current concrete enclosure around the spring was deemed unsafe, and a contest was held to design a structure that would replace it. Sculptor Frank Williams won the contest with his castle design. He named it "Seven Points" for the seven cement peaks surrounding the spring.

Arkansas & Missouri Railroad

Established in 1986, this Class III Railroad runs along a 150-mile route between Monett, Missouri, and Fort Smith, Arkansas. Its headquarters are located in Springdale, Arkansas, but major operations are out of Fort Smith. The train is more than just a tourist attraction, as it carries freight between Springdale and Fort Smith, but it primarily acts as a window to the past for passengers who take the full 150-mile trip through the Ozark Mountains. The train also works with numerous businesses throughout the valley to carry freight and provide storage. It also hauls sand for a concrete sand company in Butterfield, Missouri.

Best Time to Visit: The Arkansas & Missouri Railroad operates year-round, although some months are on a limited basis. The best time to visit is in the summer.

Pass/Permit/Fees: The rates to ride the Arkansas & Missouri Railroad vary based on distance and the car you select.

Closest City or Town: Fort Smith

How to Get There: From Little Rock: Take I-40 West for 159 miles to Exit 1 in Crawford County. Then, take US-64 East for 6.2 miles to the depot.

GPS Coordinates: 35.3904°N, -94.4300° W

Did You Know? The Arkansas & Missouri Railroad is one of only a few railroad lines left in the U.S. that operates both passenger and freight services. When you ride this train, you're traveling over working rails since the train is conducting business along the way.

Arkansas Valley

This swath of land lies between the Ouachita Mountains in the south and the Ozark Mountains in the north. It generally runs parallel to the Arkansas River and is often referred to as the Arkansas River Valley. The largest city in the Arkansas Valley is Fort Smith, but Van Buren, Ozark, Clarksville, Russellville, Dardanelle, Conway, and Heber Springs, among others, are also located in the area. The valley is 40 miles wide in places. It's known for its incredible views and unique geological features. Three of the most iconic mountains in Arkansas—Petit Jean Mountain, Mount Magazine, and Mount Nebo—are situated in the valley.

Best Time to Visit: If you're not trekking to a waterfall and you don't want to ride the rapids, fall is the best time to visit the Arkansas Valley since the temperatures are milder and the days are sunny.

Pass/Permit/Fees: There is no fee to visit the Arkansas Valley, but some attractions will require separate admission fees.

Closest City or Town: Fort Smith

How to Get There: From Little Rock: Take I-40 West for 157 miles to Grand Avenue in Fort Smith.

GPS Coordinates: 39.7768° N, -104.9119° W

Did You Know? The Arkansas Valley serves as a migration corridor for many species of birds, including ducks, geese, pelicans, and swallows, as they travel from north to south in the fall and back again in the spring.

Chaffee Barbershop Museum

The Fort Chaffee Barbershop was the place where thousands of young men who enlisted in the U.S. Army visited to get their signature buzz cut. However, no potential soldier who walked in the doors of this barbershop drew as much attention as Elvis Presley, who famously received his G.I. haircut from a barber at Fort Chaffee Barbershop on March 25, 1958. While many pundits worried that Presley's decision to enter the service would mean the end of his popularity as a rock 'n' roll star, he actually became even more beloved because of his patriotism and positive attitude. The museum, which opened in 2008, draws visitors from all over the world to tour the 1950s-era barbershop that replicates exactly what Presley saw when he sat down for his buzz cut over 60 years ago.

Best Time to Visit: The museum is open Monday through Saturday between the hours of 9:00 a.m. and 4:00 p.m.

Pass/Permit/Fees: The museum is free to visit.

Closest City or Town: Fort Smith

How to Get There: From Little Rock: Take I-40 West for 153 miles to Riggs Drive in Van Buren. Take Exit 3, and travel for 10.4 miles on State Highway 59 South to the museum.

GPS Coordinates: 35.3126° N, -94.3012° W

Did You Know? The facility is home to the Museum of Chaffee County, which includes the largest collection of artifacts from Fort Chaffee in the U.S.

Creekmore Park

This downtown park is situated across the street from the Fort Smith Public Library and provides visitors with various seasonal activities that are unique to the area. Of particular popularity is the Creekmore Express Train, which offers three miniature trains that can be ridden around the park during the warmer months of the year. There is also an Olympic-sized swimming and diving pool, a tennis center and courts, an 18-hole miniature golf course, a playground, a community center, and a fitness trail.

Best Time to Visit: The best time to visit Creekmore Park is during the summer, when all activities are open. It is recommended to check the current times and train schedules before visiting.

Pass/Permit/Fees: There is no fee to visit Creekmore Park or to ride the train. Donations are appreciated.

Closest City or Town: Fort Smith

How to Get There: From Little Rock: Take I-40 West for 159 miles to Arkansas State Highway 22 West/Rogers Avenue in Fort Smith. Take Exit 8A, and continue on Arkansas 22 for 2.4 miles to the park's entrance.

GPS Coordinates: 35.3728° N, -94.3970° W

Did You Know? The Creekmore Holiday Express train runs from December 3 through December 22 from 5:30 p.m. to 8:30 p.m. It features a journey through the park, which is adorned with hundreds of holiday lights.

Fort Smith Brewing Company

This local brewery is committed to providing the Fort Smith community with delicious beer and a relaxing taproom in which to discover their favorite brew. As the only brewery in Fort Smith, the spotlight is on the house concoctions, but the company also offers guest taps from breweries around the state. Along with thc taproom, the Curbside Comfort Café is available to provide scrumptious food to pair with your craft beer. Children are welcome in the brewery, as they have non-alcoholic beverages available along with a family-friendly atmosphere.

Best Time to Visit: The brewery is open Tuesday through Thursday from 5:00 p.m. to 10:00 p.m., Friday and Saturday from 12:00 p.m. to 10:00 p.m., and Sunday from 12:00 p.m. to 8:00 p.m. Since it's indoors, you can comfortably visit the brewery any time of the year.

Pass/Permit/Fees: There is no fee to visit the Fort Smith Brewing Company, but be sure to bring money if you want a beer or a meal.

Closest City or Town: Fort Smith

How to Get There: From Little Rock: Take I-40 West for 153 miles to Riggs Drive in Van Buren. Take Exit 3 onto Arkansas State Highway 59 South, then travel for 10.3 miles to reach the brewery.

GPS Coordinates: 35.3111° N, -94.2997° W

Did You Know? The brewery also offers special events, such as Brewery Comedy Nights and the 3rd Annual Turkey Wobble.

Fort Smith Farmers Market

If you're looking for fresh, locally grown produce, handmade candy, homemade baked goods, canned preserves and jams, and high-quality crafts and artwork, you're sure to find what you need at the Fort Smith Farmers Market. You'll also enjoy music from local musicians, street entertainment, and booths from community organizations as you peruse the offerings at the Saturday market. More than 90 vendors set up shop on Tuesdays and Saturdays to hawk their wares, so plan to spend a few morning hours shopping for local items.

Best Time to Visit: The market is open from 7:00 a.m. to 12:00 p.m. every Tuesday through Saturday between late spring and fall. It is open on Saturdays only during winter and early spring, but if you want the best vendor selection, visit during the spring or summer.

Pass/Permit/Fees: There is no fee to visit the Fort Smith Farmers Market, but have money on hand for purchases.

Closest City or Town: Fort Smith

How to Get There: From Little Rock: Take I-40 West for 157 miles to Crawford County. Take Exit 1 onto US-64, then travel for 6.2 miles to N. 2nd Street in Fort Smith, where the market is located.

GPS Coordinates: 35.3913° N, -94.4277° W

Did You Know? The market is operated by the Market Master, a local producer who verifies that all vendors are certified as growing, making, baking, catching, or crafting their products in Arkansas.

Fort Smith Museum of History

Once known as the Old Commissary Museum, the Fort Smith Museum of History is dedicated to preserving approximately 40,000 items related to the area's history. It covers the fort's construction up to the turn of the 21st century. The commissary building was built in 1906 to house Atkinson-Williams Hardware and was eventually restored as part of the Fort Smith National Historic Site. You'll find exhibits related to the 1817 fort, the story of Darby's Rangers (the forerunners of the Army Rangers), and *On the Air*, which documents the history of radio and television broadcasting in the region.

Best Time to Visit: The museum is open Tuesday through Saturday from 10:00 a.m. to 4:00 p.m.

Pass/Permit/Fees: Adult admission is $7 per person and $2 for children between the ages of 6 and 15. Veterans and active military are $5 each, and children under six years old are free.

Closest City or Town: Fort Smith

How to Get There: From Little Rock: Take I-40 West for 157 miles to Crawford County. Take Exit 1 onto US-64 East, and travel 6.3 miles to Rogers Avenue in Fort Smith, where the museum is located.

GPS Coordinates: 35.3884° N, -94.4283° W

Did You Know? On the second floor of the museum, be sure to view the collection of 19th-century woodworking tools and a display featuring the Goldman Hotel in downtown Fort Smith.

Fort Smith National Historic Site

This 1817 historic fort was the gateway to the frontier and Native American territory, making it a confluence of soldiers, settlers, and businessmen. The fort was initially constructed to broker peace between the Osage and Cherokee Indians but was abandoned in 1824 when the U.S. Army built Fort Gibson further west in Oklahoma. Eventually, due to the increasing tensions between the Native Americans and white settlers following the Indian Removal Act of 1830, a second Fort Smith was constructed in 1838 near the ruins of the original fort. The fort served as a supply depot for other forts located in Native American territory and was a major stop for the Cherokee and Choctaw Indians on the Trail of Tears.

Best Time to Visit: The Fort Smith National Historic Site is open from sunrise to sunset every day of the week. The gallows and commissary are open from 9:00 a.m. to 5:00 p.m., Monday through Friday.

Pass/Permit/Fees: There is a $10 per person walk-in fee to visit the Fort Smith National Historic Site.

Closest City or Town: Fort Smith

How to Get There: From Little Rock: Take I-40 West for 147 miles to Crawford County. Take Exit 1 onto US-64 East, and travel for 6.4 miles to Parker Avenue in Fort Smith, where the site is located.

GPS Coordinates: 35.3887° N, -94.4296° W

Did You Know? In 1863, Union troops captured the fort from Confederate forces.

Fort Smith Regional Art Museum

Originally the Fort Smith Art Center, the Associated Artists of Fort Smith founded what would become the Fort Smith Regional Art Museum in 1960. For 50 years, it was a space for local and regional artists to display their work. However, when the new 16,000 square-foot museum opened in 2009, it became a nationally recognized museum that facilitates national and international art exhibits alongside the works of local and regional artists. Additionally, art classes are available for children and adults, along with lectures, art camps, galas, school programs, receptions, and artist-led workshops.

Best Time to Visit: The Fort Smith Regional Art Museum is open Tuesday through Saturday from 11:00 a.m. to 6:00 p.m. and on Sunday from 1:00 p.m. to 5:00 p.m.

Pass/Permit/Fees: There is no fee to visit the Fort Smith Regional Art Museum, but donations are appreciated.

Closest City or Town: Fort Smith

How to Get There: From Little Rock: Take I-40 West for 157 miles to Grand Avenue in Fort Smith. Then, take Exit 6 onto Grand Avenue, and travel for 3.1 miles to Rogers Avenue, where the museum is located.

GPS Coordinates: 35.3819° N, -94.4156° W

Did You Know? The museum has received the Preservation through Rehabilitation Award and the American Society of Interior Designers Gold Award.

Fort Smith Trolley Museum

In 1985, the Fort Smith Streetcar Restoration Association built a car barn to house its collection of trolley cars, which were in various states of restoration. This eventually led to the founding of the Fort Smith Trolley Museum. The barn's signature feature is the three sets of front doors, which were removed from the old Frisco roundhouse when it was slated for demolition. An additional building was later purchased on South Third Street. It added 6,000 square feet to the museum for the storage of vehicles waiting for restoration. A restored Kansas City Birney Car, #1545, gives visitors authentic trolley rides from the museum to Ross Pendergraft Park and back.

Best Time to Visit: The trolley operates from 12:00 p.m. to 5:00 p.m., Tuesday through Friday, and from 10:00 a.m. to 5:00 p.m. on Saturday. On Sunday, it's available from 1:00 p.m. to 5:00 p.m. The museum itself is only open on Saturday from 10:00 a.m. to 5:00 p.m.

Pass/Permit/Fees: Trolley rides are $4 for adults and $2 for children.

Closest City or Town: Fort Smith

How to Get There: From Little Rock: Take I-40 West for 156 miles to Kelley Highway in Fort Smith. Take Exit 5 onto Kelley Highway, and travel for 4.2 miles to N. 6th Street, where the museum is located.

GPS Coordinates: 35.3865° N, -94.4302° W

Did You Know? Visitors are able to watch as the cars are restored to their former glory right before their eyes.

Janet Huckabee Arkansas River Valley Nature Center

Located on 170 acres of what used to be Fort Chaffee, the Janet Huckabee Arkansas River Valley Nature Center is home to several hiking trails and Wells Lake, an excellent place for fishing or kayaking. In addition to the various wildlife that you're likely to see along a hike, you can visit several exhibits in the nature center itself. These include reproductions of the Ozark and Ouachita Mountains; a life-sized oak tree, complete with game and non-game animals; and a 1,200-gallon aquarium that showcases fish native to Arkansas.

Best Time to Visit: The center is open from 8:30 a.m. to 4:30 p.m., Tuesday through Saturday. Activities on the lake are great for summer visits, but the center can comfortably be visited all year.

Pass/Permit/Fees: There is no fee to visit the Janet Huckabee Arkansas River Valley Nature Center.

Closest City or Town: Fort Smith

How to Get There: From Little Rock: Take I-40 West for 159 miles to Arkansas State Highway 22 East/Rogers Avenue in Fort Smith. Take Exit 8B onto Rogers Avenue, then drive 5.2 miles to the center's location.

GPS Coordinates: 35.3036° N, -94.3368° W

Did You Know? The center has a classroom that is used for educational programs like the Arkansas Game & Fish Commission's Boating Safety and Hunter Safety programs.

Massard Prairie Battlefield Park

Union troops and locals often used Massard Prairie as a grazing ground for their horses, but on July 27, 1864, 800 Confederate soldiers launched a surprise attack against the 200 Union soldiers stationed there. It became one of the most successful Confederate attacks on Union soldiers in Arkansas. The site exists today as a memorial to the men who died during the battle. You'll tour four main areas of the Union camp, which are the kitchen (mess area), the Parade Ground, and the camps of companies B and D. Additionally, there are historical markers, a memorial flagstaff, a monument, and a walking trail at the park.

Best Time to Visit: This attraction is outside, so the best time to visit is during summer and fall when the weather is warm and dry.

Pass/Permit/Fees: There is no fee to visit Massard Prairie Battlefield Park.

Closest City or Town: Fort Smith

How to Get There: From Little Rock: Take I-40 West for 162 miles to Arkansas Highway 255 South/S. Zero Street in Sebastian County. Take Exit 11 onto Arkansas 255 South to reach State Highway 45. Travel 2 miles to Morgans Way, where the park is located.

GPS Coordinates: 35.3127° N, -94.3822° W

Did You Know? Numerous Native American troops from the Cherokee, Creek, Choctaw, Chickasaw, and Seminole nations joined the Confederate forces during the surprise attack on the Union soldiers.

Miss Laura's Visitor Center

Known locally as Miss Laura's Social Club, the Miss Laura's Visitor Center is one of seven houses that populated the red-light district in Fort Smith during the early 1900s. It's the only "house of ill repute" that still stands, and it's now the only brothel listed on the National Register of Historic Places. The ladies offered at Miss Laura's house were reputed to be the "healthiest and most sophisticated in Fort Smith," making it one of the most well-known bordellos in the southwest. By 1910, the brothel business waned as Fort Smith residents worked to remove the red-light district. Laura Ziegler, who purchased the house in 1898, sold it to "Big Bertha" in 1911.

Best Time to Visit: Miss Laura's Visitor Center is open Monday through Saturday from 9:00 a.m. to 4:00 p.m. and Sunday from 1:00 p.m. to 4:30 p.m.

Pass/Permit/Fees: There is no fee to visit.

Closest City or Town: Fort Smith

How to Get There: From Little Rock: Take I-40 West for 156 miles to Kelley Highway in Fort Smith. Take Exit 5 onto Kelley Highway, then travel for 4.1 miles to N. B Street, where the house is located.

GPS Coordinates: 35.3930° N, -94.4292° W

Did You Know? On January 7, 1910, a storage tank exploded in the red-light district, causing two houses to burn to the ground and sending women and their customers running. This was known locally as the "night of the lingerie parade."

Parrot Island Waterpark

Parrot Island Waterpark features a variety of water activities, including a wave pool, water slides, cabana rentals, and more. The only two-lake FlowRider and wave pool in Arkansas is located at Parrot Island Waterpark. Other amazing attractions include the brand-new O'Hana Highway, the Crocodile Creek Lazy River, the Pineapple Plunge, the Blue Macaw, the Tangerine Twist, the Caribbean Splash, Toucan's Cove Activity Pool, and the Tiny Turtle Island Kiddie Pool.

Best Time to Visit: The best time to visit is in the summer. The park is open from at least 11:00 a.m. (sometimes 10:00 a.m.) to at least 6:00 p.m. (sometimes 7:00 p.m.) from mid-May through October. Check the website for actual operating hours before your visit.

Pass/Permit/Fees: The fee for guests over 48" tall is $18. Guests under 48" tall are $13. Children ages three and under are free.

Closest City or Town: Fort Smith

How to Get There: From the north or south: Take I-540 to Exit 11. Exit onto Zero Street. Turn left (if from coming from the north) or right (if coming from the south). Drive for 2.25 miles, and you'll see Parrot Island on the right.

GPS Coordinates: 35.3257° N, -94.3520° W

Did You Know? The Parrot Island Waterpark pumps more than 400,000 gallons of water through its numerous water attractions.

Saint Scholastica Monastery

Saint Scholastica Monastery is a community of Catholic Benedictine nuns that has had a presence in Fort Smith for over a hundred years. The monastery has significantly impacted the region through their contributions to the education, healthcare, and social needs of the city and beyond. They have provided staffing for three all-girl high schools (the Institute of St. Scholastica, St. Joseph Academy, and St. Scholastica Academy), operated four rural hospitals, and cared for infants and children in several area orphanages between 1932 and 1997. Dozens of sisters live in the monastery, providing services to nursing homes, prisons, and other social facilities.

Best Time to Visit: The monastery's gift shop is open 9:00 a.m. to 12:00 p.m. on Monday, Wednesday, and Friday, but appointments must be scheduled in advance.

Pass/Permit/Fees: There is no fee to visit the Saint Scholastica Monastery.

Closest City or Town: Fort Smith

How to Get There: From Little Rock: Take I-40 West for 159 miles to Arkansas Highway 22 West/Rogers Avenue in Fort Smith. Take Exit 8A onto Arkansas 22 West. Drive for 1.4 miles to S. 42nd Street/S. Albert Pike Avenue, where the monastery is located.

GPS Coordinates: 35.3712° N, -94.3858° W

Did You Know? The founding sisters of Saint Scholastica were lured to Arkansas from Indiana by the promise of 100 acres of land and $2,500 to build a school and a church.

The Clayton House

This gorgeous Victorian mansion was the home of William Henry Harrison Clayton and his family beginning in 1882. During this time, Clayton served as the U.S. Attorney for the federal Western District of Arkansas. In 1969, the home was slated for demolition, but Fort Smith residents banded together to create the Fort Smith Heritage Foundation to save the house and preserve its history. It reopened as a museum in 1977, treating visitors to coal-burning fireplaces, period furnishings, and elegant woodwork from the late 19th century.

Best Time to Visit: The museum is open from 12:00 p.m. to 4:00 p.m., Tuesday through Saturday, and from 1:00 p.m. to 4:00 p.m. on Sunday. You can also visit the house by appointment.

Pass/Permit/Fees: There is no fee to visit the Clayton House, but there is a suggested donation of $6 for adults, $5 for seniors, and $3 for children ages 6 through 17 if you decide to take the 50-minute tour.

Closest City or Town: Fort Smith

How to Get There: From Little Rock: Take I-40 West for 157 miles to Kelley Highway in Fort Smith. Take Exit 5 onto Kelley Highway, and drive for 3.5 miles to N. 6th Street, where the house is located.

GPS Coordinates: 35.3923° N, -94.4208° W

Did You Know? Artifacts such as Clayton's family Bible, Mr. Clayton's walking stick, and Mrs. Clayton's writing table are also on display in the home.

The Park at West End

This downtown park is a throwback to the 1935 World's Fair, with an authentic Ferris wheel and a vintage carousel that was hand-painted in Treviso, Italy. You'll also enjoy a refurbished Pullman Railcar Diner, a concession stand converted from a double-decker bus, and a modern LED-lighted splash pad for anyone who wants to cool off in the hot Arkansas summers. For visitors who are also art lovers, you'll be entranced by the original artwork of D*Face, an artist from the United Kingdom.

Best Time to Visit: Between late April and late May, and mid-August to late October, the park is open on Friday from 4:00 p.m. to 9:00 p.m. and on Saturday from 10:00 a.m. to 9:00 p.m. Between late May to mid-August, it's open from 1:00 p.m. to 9:00 p.m., Tuesday through Thursday, from 1:00 p.m. to 10:00 p.m. on Friday, and from 10:00 a.m. to 10:00 p.m. on Saturday.

Pass/Permit/Fees: There is no fee to visit the Park at West End, but it will cost $1 per person to ride the Ferris wheel.

Closest City or Town: Fort Smith

How to Get There: From Little Rock: Take I-40 West for 159 miles to Exit 1 in Crawford County. Take US-64 East for 6.1 miles to Belle Point Drive in Fort Smith, where the park is located.

GPS Coordinates: 35.3915° N, -94.4288° W

Did You Know? The park's owners will only sell or change the park's hands under the condition the park operations are kept the same.

Spring River

Spring River emerges near the Missouri border in north-central Arkansas. It is a crystal-clear stream that provides some of the cleanest fresh water in the state. This river is popular with anglers, especially those who are fishing for walleye and trout, but fly fishing is also popular in areas of the upper river. If you're looking to cool off during the summer, this river offers an excellent place to float, even during the months when most rivers run low. The river remains cold all year because its source is Mammoth Spring, which releases 9 million gallons of 58°F water every hour.

Best Time to Visit: Summer is the best time to visit Spring River because of its constantly cool temperatures. It may be too cold for water activities in other seasons.

Pass/Permit/Fees: There is no cost to visit Spring River, but if you need to rent a canoe or kayak, there will be a rental fee.

Closest City or Town: Hardy

How to Get There: From Little Rock: Take I-30 for 2.2 miles to US-167 North/US-67 North. Continue for 108 miles to Arkansas 58 in Cave City. Follow Arkansas 58 to Campbell Road. Drive for 28.3 miles to the parking areas for the river.

GPS Coordinates: 36.2358° N, -91.1545° W

Did You Know? Guided fishing trips are available on Spring River. You just might catch a trophy fish, like a Tiger Muskie or champion bass.

Buffalo National River

One of the few remaining undammed rivers in the United States, the Buffalo National River offers 135 miles of free-flowing water. Along the way down the river, travelers will encounter both wild rapids and calm pools surrounded by the towering bluffs of the Ozark Mountains. Some stretches of the river are available for kayaking, while others are too dangerous for even the most accomplished paddlers. Hiking and camping are also available in the area.

Best Time to Visit: The upper river between Ponca and Pruitt is crowded during April and May, and the middle and lower river sections are busier during June and July.

Pass/Permit/Fees: Buffalo National River is free to visit, but if you want to float down the river, you will need to rent a raft or kayak from a local tour company if you don't have your own.

Closest City or Town: Harrison

How to Get There: From Harrison: Take Highway 7 South to the Upper District in Jasper or Ponca. Take Highway 65 for 31 miles to Tyler Bend to reach the Middle District. To reach the lower district, take Highway 65 for 5 miles to Highway 62/412 East to Yellville. Then, take Highway 14 to Buffalo Point.

GPS Coordinates: 35.9829° N, -92.7548° W

Did You Know? In 1972, the Buffalo River became the first river in the U.S. to receive the national river designation. It begins in the Boston Mountains and ends in the Ozark Mountains.

Crystal Dome

This cave is the second of two located in the area, with its entrance fewer than 400 feet from Mystic Caverns, which is also covered in this book. It was discovered when a heavy equipment operator broke through the surface and found the hollow interior. Crystal Dome is one of the best-preserved caves in the world and has only been open to the public since 1982.

Best Time to Visit: As with the Mystic Caverns, the best time to visit is during the summer; however, Crystal Dome is open year-round, weather permitting.

Pass/Permit/Fees: Adult admission is $15.99, and children between the ages of 4 and 12 are $9.99. Both caves can be toured for a price of $22.99 for adults and $12.99 for children ages 4–12.

Closest City or Town: Harrison

How to Get There: From Harrison: Take Highway 7 South toward Jasper for 7.3 miles. Turn right on Caverns Drive to arrive at Crystal Dome.

GPS Coordinates: 36.1196° N, -93.1266° W

Did You Know? The Crystal Dome is known for its 70-foot-tall dome known as the "Crystal Bell." Once you reach the bottom of the Crystal Dome, you are 110 feet below the Earth's surface.

Lost Valley Trail

One of the most popular river trails in the Buffalo National River area, Lost Valley Trail features incredible geology, wonderful waterfalls, intriguing caves, and a gorgeous riverside setting. The hike through the box canyon carved by Clark Creek is moderately difficult, but the scenery is worth the extra effort. Approximately 1 mile along the Lost Valley Trail, you'll come across Eden Falls, a 53-foot, two-tiered waterfall that flows softly into the pool at the base of the canyon. This location is perfect for a family with older children who can handle a longer hike.

Best Time to Visit: As this trail gets crowded on the weekends, it's best to visit during the week if you prefer a more peaceful hike. In the spring, the waterfall will flow more swiftly, but the hike is great at any time of the year.

Pass/Permit/Fees: There is no fee to visit the Lost Valley Trail.

Closest City or Town: Harrison

How to Get There: From Harrison: Take Arkansas Highway 43 South for 22 miles. Turn right and travel 1 mile to reach the trailhead.

GPS Coordinates: 36.0101° N, -93.3743° W

Did You Know? At the end of the trail, you'll find Cobb Cave, which is open to the public for exploration. The entrance looks small for about 200 feet, but it opens up into a large room that features a 35-foot waterfall. Bring a flashlight if you intend to explore the cave because there is no natural or man-made light source.

Mystic Caverns

Originally named Mansion Cave due to the massive calcite formations in the underground chamber, Mystic Cavern offers a glimpse at rare calcite formations like shields, helictites, and spherical stalactites. The 45-minute tour will take you along the path of Arkansas's first settlers and teach you about the infamous "pipe organ" and "spider monkey" inside the caves.

Best Time to Visit: While the caverns are open year-round (from 9:00 a.m. to 5:00 in the summer, fall, and spring, and from 9:00 a.m. to 4:00 p.m. in the winter), the best time of year to visit is in the summer.

Pass/Permit/Fees: Adult admission is $18.99, while children between the ages of 4 and 12 are $11.99.

Closest City or Town: Harrison

How to Get There: From Harrison: Take Highway 7 South toward Jasper for 7.3 miles. Turn right on Caverns Drive to arrive at Mystic Caverns

GPS Coordinates: 36.1196° N, -93.1266° W

Did You Know? Mystic Caverns has been open to the public for tours since the late 1920s. After the Onyx Cave, it was the second cave to be commercially operated in the state.

Little Red River

Anglers looking to catch rainbow, cutthroat, or brown trout love the Little Red River, which emerges from beneath the Greers Ferry Lake dam. The icy cold water is not suitable for swimming, but if fishing is your game, this is one of the most popular fishing spots in the state. Hiking is available around the river, and there are several resort villages that surround the lake. You can also rent a boat from the full-service marinas in the area and spend time exploring the massive, 35-mile river.

Best Time to Visit: The brown trout spawning season is from mid-October through November, making this the ideal time to fish in the Little Red River.

Pass/Permit/Fees: There is no fee to visit the Little Red River, but a fishing license is required if you intend to fish, and boat rental rates vary.

Closest City or Town: Heber Springs

How to Get There: From Little Rock: Take US-167 North/US-67 North for 53.8 miles to Exit 48 (Arkansas 385) in White County. Turn north on Arkansas 385. Continue for 10.5 miles to House Road, then take House Road to the Little Red River.

GPS Coordinates: 35.6536° N, -92.3191° W

Did You Know? In 1992, Howard "Rip" Collins set the world record for a brown trout with his 40-pound, 4-ounce fish that he caught out of the Little Red River.

Garvan Woodland Gardens

Located in the Ouachita Mountains, the Garvan Woodland Gardens provide visitors with a pristine example of Arkansas's incredible diversity of flora and fauna. Verna Cook Garvan developed the Woodland Gardens as part of her private residence for more than 40 years. In fact, there are hundreds of trees and shrubs that are more than four decades old, including some rare magnolias and camellias. When Ms. Garvan died in 1993, she bequeathed the gardens to the University of Arkansas Foundation, which allowed them to continue to grow under the guidance of the Fay Jones School of Architecture.

Best Time to Visit: The gardens are open from 10:00 a.m. to 6:00 p.m. every day of the week. The best time to visit is spring and early summer to see the flowers in bloom.

Pass/Permit/Fees: Adult admission is $15 per person. Children between the ages of 4 and 12 are $5.00, and children ages three and under are free. Dogs are $5 each and must be on short, non-retractable leashes.

Closest City or Town: Hot Springs

How to Get There: From Little Rock: Take I-30 West to Exit 111, then take US-70 West. Take Exit 6 onto Highway 128/Carpenter Dam Road. Turn left and travel 4 miles to Arkridge Road. Turn right onto Arkridge Road, and continue for 1.1 miles to the gardens' entrance.

GPS Coordinates: 34.4369° N, -93.0482° W

Did You Know? The gardens feature over 160 types of azaleas, many of which were planted by Ms. Garvin.

Hot Springs National Park

Known as Bathhouse Row, the bathhouses in Hot Springs National Park are heated by Hot Springs Creek, which runs directly through the park. Originally, the bathhouses were constructed of canvas and lumber, and resembled crude tents hovering over springs or reservoirs. In 1896, wooden bathhouses began to replace the primitive structures of the past. Today, visitors can experience the ancient thermal springs in more modern bathhouses while enjoying spectacular mountain views and fascinating geology.

Best Time to Visit: Since the springs provide warm water, the baths are pleasant during the cooler months of the year. Early spring and late fall are the most crowded months, but also the most comfortable for soaking in the springs.

Pass/Permit/Fees: Hot Springs National Park is free to visit unless you're staying overnight. Camping costs about $30 per night, but contact the park directly for current rates and availability.

Closest City or Town: Hot Springs

How to Get There: From Little Rock: Take I-30 West to US-70 West. Take Exit 111 toward Hot Springs. Turn right onto Spring Street, then right again onto Central Avenue. Arrive at Hot Springs National Park.

GPS Coordinates: 34.5217° N, -93.0424° W

Did You Know? In addition to the bathhouses, there are 26 miles of hiking trails available in the park, so plan to spend more than one day exploring this incredible area.

Lake Catherine State Park

Lake Catherine is one of the five lakes located within the Ouachita Mountain range. It offers fishing, boating, hiking, guided horseback riding, and more. There are 20 fully equipped cabins that offer private access to the lake and include their own fishing pier. There are also 70 campsites on the property and six primitive tent sites. A small, but picturesque waterfall can be reached from a well-marked hiking trail that is both family and pet friendly.

Best Time to Visit: This is one of the busiest parks in the Arkansas state park system, especially in the summer. If you plan to boat or swim, you may want to choose late spring or early fall.

Pass/Permit/Fees: There is no fee to visit Lake Catherine unless you stay overnight. Cabin rates start at $200 per night, and campsites start at $13 per night for a tent site.

Closest City or Town: Hot Springs

How to Get There: From Little Rock: Take I-430 South and I-30 West to Arkansas 84 in Malvern. Take Exit 97 from I-30 West, then travel 44.3 miles to Arkansas 171. Go north on Arkansas 171, and travel 9.7 miles to reach the park's entrance.

GPS Coordinates: 34.4287° N, -92.9226° W

Did You Know? Lake Catherine served as a rest and recreation facility for wounded servicemen who were at the nearby Army-Navy Hospital in Hot Springs between 1942 and 1945.

Lake Ouachita

With 40,000 acres of water, Lake Ouachita is the largest lake in the state. It is an angler's paradise, with plenty of opportunities to catch crappie, catfish, bream, striped bass, and largemouth bass. In addition to the four cabins on the property, there are 93 campsites that can accommodate RVs and tents. Some of these campsites are right next to the water. Hiking, swimming, kayaking, and other activities are also available in the park.

Best Time to Visit: The best time to fish at Lake Ouachita is between March and May, but the park is open all year. Summer is the most crowded.

Pass/Permit/Fees: There is no cost to visit Lake Ouachita unless you plan to stay overnight or store your boat at the marina.

Closest City or Town: Hot Springs Village

How to Get There: From Hot Springs Village, head west on Fresno toward Carmona Drive. Turn right onto Alicante Road, and take a slight left toward E. Villena. Continue on E. Villena, then take a left onto DeSoto Boulevard. Turn right onto AR-7 North/N. State Highway 7. Turn left onto Arkansas 298 West. Continue on Buckville Road, and drive to Tadpole Point.

GPS Coordinates: 34.5902° N, -93.3439° W

Did You Know? Eagle tours are available at Lake Ouachita State Park in the winter when the birds are staying in the area.

Sam's Throne

While Sam's Throne is primarily known for rock climbing opportunities, it is also a popular location for camping, hiking, and photography. It is located on Judea Mountain and overlooks the Big Creek valley below. Whether you're just beginning to rock climb or you're an expert, there are challenging climbs for all skill levels, especially for those who are into top roping. For a picturesque hike, take the 2.5-mile loop hiking trail that begins near the main parking lot. The campsites are primitive and mostly used by rock climbers. RVs will not be able to negotiate the steep road leading to Sam's Throne.

Best Time to Visit: Sam's Throne is available to visit year round, but it gets crowded on weekends, especially in the warmer months. For a more pleasant experience, try to visit during the week.

Pass/Permit/Fees: There is no fee to access Sam's Throne, even for camping.

Closest City or Town: Jasper

How to Get There: From Jasper: Take Arkansas Highway 74 East for 9.7 miles to Arkansas Highway 123. Turn south on Highway 123/74, and travel 4.5 miles to Mt. Judea. At the 123/74 split, turn right on. Continue on Arkansas Highway 123 for 4.3 miles to reach the entrance.

GPS Coordinates: 35.8711° N, -93.0524° W

Did You Know? There are more than 300 rock climbing routes on Sam's Throne, which is why it is popular with rock climbers of all abilities.

Moro Bay

A popular fishing area, Moro Bay is one of two lakes that join the Ouachita River. If you're looking for a camping spot that offers some of the best fishing in Arkansas, this is the place for you. It offers superior cabins, 23 Class AAA campsites, and a marina with slip and boat rentals. There is even a store that provides gas, basic groceries, and gifts. All cabins have two bedrooms, two bathrooms, a kitchen, and a screened deck to enjoy the views of Moro Bay.

Best Time to Visit: The peak season for Moro Bay is May through September, but even then, the park is so large that it doesn't feel crowded. Be sure to rent your cabin early, though, as they do go fast.

Pass/Permit/Fees: Moro Bay is free to visit unless you're staying overnight. Camping starts at $36 per night, and cabins start at $142 per night.

Closest City or Town: Jersey

How to Get There: From Little Rock: Take I-530 South and US-63 South to Highway 600 South in Jersey. Turn right onto Highway 600 South, and travel less than a mile to the park's entrance.

GPS Coordinates: 33.3065° N, -92.3504° W

Did You Know? While at Moro Bay, check out the Moro Bay Ferry exhibit that features a display of a tugboat and barge that were used to cross the Ouachita River from 1828 to 1948 and again from 1965 to 1992. These boats were built in 1948. They're the last ferry boats in Arkansas that were used by the public.

Centennial Bank Stadium

Originally named the Indian Stadium, then ASU Stadium, then Liberty Bank Stadium, Centennial Bank Stadium is located on the Arkansas State University campus. It's where the Red Wolves collegiate football team plays. It has a capacity of 30,406 spectators following several renovations in the 1990s and early 2000s that added bleacher seats, luxury suites, and box seats to the stadium. The facility held its first game in 1974, but the stadium was not completely finished until later. In the beginning, it only held 16,343 fans. In addition to spectator seats, the stadium also boasts two donor levels, a photo deck, a visiting team athletic director suite, coaches' booths, and a million-dollar video scoreboard, added in 2001.

Best Time to Visit: Visit Centennial Bank Stadium during football season in the fall and early winter.

Pass/Permit/Fees: The cost to visit Centennial Bank Stadium is dependent upon seat selection.

Closest City or Town: Jonesboro

How to Get There: From Little Rock: Take US-67 North for 109 miles to Arkansas State Highway 226 East in Craighead County. Take Exit 102 onto Arkansas 226, then continue for 23.7 miles to reach the stadium in Jonesboro.

GPS Coordinates: 35.8498° N, -90.6669° W

Did You Know? The attendance record at Centennial Bank Stadium was set on December 1, 2012, when 31,243 fans saw the Red Wolves defeat Middle Tennessee State University with a score of 45–0.

Craighead Forest Park

Located in Crowley's Ridge, Craighead Forest Park is a 692-acre recreational area that provides facilities for basketball, bird watching, disc golfing, biking, running, fishing, and more. There are playgrounds for children and a dog jumping pier. The lake is regularly stocked with bream, bass, tilapia, and crappie, which makes this a popular location for serious anglers. Pay laundry machines, and a bathhouse with showers and flush toilets are recent additions to the 26-site campground in the park. If you'd rather not have the convenience of water and electrical hookups, there are also tent sites and primitive camping areas available as well.

Best Time to Visit: Summer is the best time to visit the park for water activities, but spring and fall offer excellent fishing opportunities.

Pass/Permit/Fees: There is no fee to visit Craighead Forest Park, but if you decide to stay at the campground, there will be a camping cost.

Closest City or Town: Jonesboro

How to Get There: From Little Rock: Take US-67 North for 109 miles to Arkansas State Highway 226 East in Craighead County. Take Exit 102, then drive for 20.1 miles to reach the park's entrance.

GPS Coordinates: 35.7823° N, -90.7022° W

Did You Know? Craighead Forest Park dates back to 1937 when the Young Men's Civic Club created the lake as a community project.

Forrest L. Wood Crowley's Ridge Nature Center

This 17,033-square-foot nature center opened on August 25, 2004. It features 160 acres of prairie land, ponds, and woodlands at the southern boundary of Craighead Forest Park. The facility itself is three stories of educational exhibits and meeting space intended to further the Arkansas Game & Fish Commission's mission of conserving Arkansas's fish, wildlife, and habitats while promoting sustainable use of the land. The Habitats Trail takes visitors around Willow Pond, across a ridge top and levee, and to the prairie's edge before returning to the center.

Best Time to Visit: The Forrest L. Wood Crowley's Ridge Nature Center is open between 8:30 a.m. and 4:30 p.m., Tuesday through Saturday.

Pass/Permit/Fees: There is no fee to visit the Forrest L. Wood Crowley's Ridge Nature Center.

Closest City or Town: Jonesboro

How to Get There: Take US-67 North for 109 miles to Arkansas State Highway 226 East in Craighead County. Take Exit 102, then drive for 18.9 miles to reach the park's entrance.

GPS Coordinates: 35.7683° N, -90.7046° W

Did You Know? In the center, you'll find several interactive exhibits and a 16-minute film to watch. The Crow's Nest on the third floor gives visitors a bird's eye view of Crowley's Ridge.

Lake Frierson State Park

Year-round fishing is the main attraction of Lake Frierson State Park, where anglers can find catfish, saugeye, bass, bream, and crappie in any season. There are seven campsites at the park—all Class B with electric and water hookups—and three no-hookup tent sites. A playground, fishing pier, and hiking trails round out the activities available in this park. You can also view several nature exhibits at the visitor center or rent a fishing boat, pedal boat, or kayak at the bait shop.

Best Time to Visit: Fishing is good all year long, but it is a more picturesque place to visit in the spring.

Pass/Permit/Fees: There is no fee to visit Lake Frierson State Park, but a fishing license is required. Additionally, if you plan to stay overnight, a camping fee will be assessed.

Closest City or Town: Jonesboro

How to Get There: From Jonesboro: Take Cate Avenue west toward S. Main Street. Turn right onto S. Main Street. Follow this road for 8.8 miles as it turns into Arkansas Highway 141 North/N. Church Street. Turn left into the park's entrance.

GPS Coordinates: 35.9729° N, -90.7173° W

Did You Know? You will find a unique combination of forests in Lake Frierson State Park, which is rare for Arkansas. There are the forests found in the Appalachians, Ozark forests of oak and hickory, and the rarer species of northern red oak trees, tulip trees, and cucumber trees.

The Bradbury Art Museum

Originally named the Bradbury Gallery, the Bradbury Art Museum showcases contemporary art on the campus of Arkansas State University. The gallery was created in 2001 with an endowment from Curt Bradbury, who gifted the funds to the university to honor his wife, Charlotte. Its initial purpose of displaying works of contemporary art expanded over the years, and in 2015, the gallery was renamed to better represent its full mission of teaching, collecting, and presenting contemporary art.

Best Time to Visit: The museum is open Tuesday through Saturday from 12:00 p.m. to 5:00 p.m., and by appointment when the university is also open. The best time to visit is during the summer when most classes are not in session.

Pass/Permit/Fees: There is no fee to visit the Bradbury Art Museum.

Closest City or Town: Jonesboro

How to Get There: From Little Rock: Take I-30 for 2.5 miles to US-67. Follow US-67 for 107 miles to Arkansas Highway 226 in Craighead County. Take Exit 102, and continue onto Arkansas 225 for 23.7 miles to the museum's location.

GPS Coordinates: 35.8440° N, -90.6698° W

Did You Know? Each year, the museum hosts the Delta National Small Prints Exhibition, which is a nationally recognized juried print show that features both national and international artists.

The Skirmish at Jonesboro

Throughout the Civil War, Craighead County, in which the city of Jonesboro is located, was a Confederate stronghold. On August 1, 1862, Union soldiers surprised a Confederate encampment south of Jonesboro, and 14 men were taken, prisoner. These men were marched the 2 miles to Jonesboro and locked in the new county courthouse. The next day, the Confederates attacked the Union soldiers on Craighead Courthouse grounds. Seven Union soldiers and one Confederate soldier were killed, and the Confederate prisoners were freed. A memorial dedicated to this skirmish has been erected at the Jonesboro courthouse.

Best Time to Visit: The memorial is open year-round.

Pass/Permit/Fees: It is free to visit the memorial.

Closest City or Town: Jonesboro

How to Get There: From Little Rock: Take US-67 North for 109 miles to Arkansas Highway 226 East in Craighead County. Take Exit 102, and travel for 20.7 miles to S. Main Street in Jonesboro, where the courthouse and memorial are located.

GPS Coordinates: 35.8386° N, -90.7049° W

Did You Know? The Union soldiers were not expecting the Confederates to attack the courthouse, particularly at dawn. Because they were unfamiliar with the area, they were vulnerable to becoming confused during the battle, which is exactly what happened. They were run out of town, allowing the Confederates to easily free the prisoners from the county jail.

Tomlinson Stadium–Kell Field

Opened in 1993, the J.A. "Ike" Tomlinson Stadium–Kell Field is the home stadium for the Arkansas State University baseball team. In addition to the field, the facility includes an indoor workout area and batting cages. The stadium is named for Coach J.A. "Ike" Tomlinson, the Arkansas State University baseball coach from 1944 to 1976. He has been credited with getting the university's athletics program back on track after World War II. The field is named after George and Skeeter Kell, brothers who both played baseball at Arkansas State University and were drafted into the major leagues. In fact, in 1983, George Kell was inducted into the Baseball Hall of Fame.

Best Time to Visit: The best time to visit Tomlinson Stadium–Kell Field is during baseball season, which is in the spring and summer.

Pass/Permit/Fees: The fee to visit Tomlinson Stadium–Kell Field varies based on game and seat selection.

Closest City or Town: Jonesboro

How to Get There: From Little Rock: Take US-67 North for 109 miles to Arkansas State Highway 226 East in Craighead County. Take Exit 102, and drive for 23.9 miles on Arkansas 226 to the stadium.

GPS Coordinates: 35.8437° N, -90.6685° W

Did You Know? The stadium did not get lights until 1996, which meant that prior to that year, all games had to be played during the day.

Lake Chicot

Lake Chicot, located in Lake Chicot State Park, is the largest natural lake in the state. It is also the largest oxbow (U-shaped) lake in North America. Fishermen flock to this lake to take advantage of its calm, clean waters and to fish for crappie, largemouth bass, bream, striped bass, and channel catfish. Visitors can rent boats at the marina, and a seasonal swimming pool is available at an additional cost between Memorial Day and Labor Day. There are 14 cabins and 122 campsites to accommodate overnight stays.

Best Time to Visit: The park is open all year, but for anglers looking to catch crappie, bass, and bream, spring and fall are the ideal months to visit.

Pass/Permit/Fees: Lake Chicot is free to visit unless you stay overnight, visit the pool, or rent a boat. Contact the park directly for rates.

Closest City or Town: Lake Village

How to Get There: From Little Rock: Take I-530 South for 124 miles to State Highway 257. Continue for 7.7 miles to the park's entrance.

GPS Coordinates: 33.3719° N, -91.1958° W

Did You Know? The 20 miles of Lake Chicot used to be a main channel of the Mississippi River. The lake was the site of a Civil War battle in June of 1864, which was eventually won by the Union. This battle opened up the Mississippi River for travel and contributed heavily to the eventual Union victory.

Arkansas Repertory Theatre

Known colloquially as "The Rep," the Arkansas Repertory Theatre is the largest nonprofit resident theatre company in Arkansas. Guest artists and local artists work side by side to produce performances that are developed, rehearsed, and performed in Little Rock. The company focuses on stories that tell the tale of the human journey and range from modern comedies and dramas to Broadway hits and classic literature. The mission of this theatre is to entertain, educate, enrich, and engage audiences from all over Arkansas and beyond. The theatre has a stellar reputation and has been repeatedly recognized as the Best Live Theatre and Best Performing Arts Organization by the local newspapers.

Best Time to Visit: The performance season runs from May to December, but there are often special events during the other months as well.

Pass/Permit/Fees: Fees to visit the Arkansas Repertory Theatre vary by production and seat selection.

Closest City or Town: Little Rock

How to Get There: From Fort Smith: Take I-40 East for 154 miles to the I-30 Frontage Road in Little Rock. Take Exit 140 B onto US-65 South. Continue on E. 6th Street for 0.5 miles to S. Main Street, where the theatre is located.

GPS Coordinates: 34.7436° N, -92.2711° W

Did You Know? Some of the highest acclaimed productions at the theatre include *Mamma Mia!*, *August: Osage County*, and *Due South*, among many others.

Arkansas State Capitol

The structure that serves as the Arkansas State Capitol has been in place for more than 100 years. It's where six constitutional offices and the House and Senate Chambers are located. Public galleries are available. Visitors can observe their legislators as they conduct official state business. Other areas that can be toured include the Governor's Reception Room, the Rotunda, and the Old Supreme Court Chamber. The capitol building took 16 years to build, from 1899 to 1915, and cost $2.3 million, more than 1.3 million above what was initially budgeted.

Best Time to Visit: Tours are available from 8:00 a.m. to 5:00 p.m., Monday through Friday, and from 10:00 a.m. and 3:00 p.m. on Saturday.

Pass/Permit/Fees: There is no cost to visit the Arkansas State Capitol.

Closest City or Town: Little Rock

How to Get There: From Fort Smith: Take I-40 East for 156 miles to Doctor Martin Luther King, Jr. Drive in Little Rock. Take Exit 2B onto Woodlane Street, and travel for 0.4 miles to the State Capitol.

GPS Coordinates: 34.7473° N, -92.2888° W

Did You Know? The neo-classical-style capitol building, designed by architects Cass Gilbert and George Mann, was built by prison labor on the site of the former state penitentiary. The General Assembly began holding sessions in the unfinished capitol in 1911, four years before the structure would be completed.

ESSE Purse Museum

There are only three purse museums in the world, and the ESSE Purse Museum in Little Rock is the only one located in North America. Owner Anita Davis envisioned a museum that would celebrate the purse as an extension of a woman's essence, or what makes a woman "her." In fact, ESSE is derived from the Latin words for "to be." The museum aims to celebrate the American woman through the decades by examining both women's purses of choice and their contents. As such, this museum offers a combination of art, fashion, and history through various handbag displays.

Best Time to Visit: The ESSE Purse Museum is open Thursday through Saturday between 11:00 a.m. and 5:30 p.m., and on Tuesday, Wednesday, and Sunday between 11:00 a.m. and 4:00 p.m.

Pass/Permit/Fees: Adult admission is $10 per person. Students, military, and seniors are $8 per person. Children under the age of 6 are free.

Closest City or Town: Little Rock

How to Get There: From Fort Smith: Take I-40 East for 155 miles to W. 11th Street in Little Rock. Take Exit 1B, and drive 0.4 miles to Main Street, where the museum is located.

GPS Coordinates: 34.7346° N, -92.2736° W

Did You Know? The museum's permanent exhibit comprises purses from founder Anita Davis's personal extensive collection. It grew out of a traveling exhibit.

Heifer Village and Urban Farm

This educational attraction features interactive exhibits, a 3-acre urban farm modeled after heifer farms around the world, greenhouses, low-till organic gardens, and the first commercial renewable energy-operated aquaponics farm in the world. Visitors will be greeted by various farm animals, including sheep, alpacas, goats, chickens, and a cow, as they tour the working farm and discover how farming has evolved to be both sustainable and eco-friendly. A 30-minute tour of the Urban Farm will take guests through the gardens as they learn about how the organization is helping local families combat hunger and poverty. An additional 30-minute tour of Heifer Village teaches participants about how fair markets, infrastructure, and sustainable agriculture contribute to ending world poverty and hunger.

Best Time to Visit: Tours are available from 9:00 a.m. to 2:00 p.m., Monday through Friday. The mild temperatures in the spring and fall will offer the best visiting experience.

Pass/Permit/Fees: It is free, but donations are appreciated.

Closest City or Town: Little Rock

How to Get There: From Fort Smith: Take I-40 East for 154 miles to the I-30 Frontage Road in Little Rock. Take Exit 140B, then continue onto E. 6th Street for 0.6 miles to the village and farm.

GPS Coordinates: 34.7453° N, -92.2565° W

Did You Know? Other tours of the various structures on the property are available, including the Green Building Tour and the Little Farmhands Tour.

Historic Arkansas Museum

This museum is unique because it encompasses an entire city block in Little Rock. You'll find the oldest building in the city, art galleries, an 1850s farmstead, and other historical sites along the museum's path. You can even buy Arkansas-made products from local artisans. The museum is designed to preserve early Arkansas history and present the stories of the people who settled in the area through art and educational programs. The museum also hosts a variety of events throughout the year, including concerts, lectures, special art exhibits, book talks, and tours.

Best Time to Visit: The museum is open Tuesday through Saturday from 9:00 a.m. to 5:00 p.m., and on Sunday from 1:00 p.m. to 5:00 p.m. Since much of it is outside, the best time to visit is during the spring, summer, or early fall when the weather is warmer.

Pass/Permit/Fees: There is no fee to visit the Historic Arkansas Museum.

Closest City or Town: Little Rock

How to Get There: From Fort Smith: Take I-40 East for 154 miles to E. 2nd Street in Little Rock. Take Exit 141A, and travel 0.1 miles to E. 3rd Street, where the museum is located.

GPS Coordinates: 34.7468° N, -92.2693° W

Did You Know? The museum's permanent collections include period furniture, guns, jewelry, knives, hunting horns, pottery, quilts, paintings, and silver artifacts like spoons.

Little Rock Central High School National Historic Site

Visit the epicenter of the school integration battle of the 1950s, when the U.S. Supreme Court mandated that public schools allow Black students to attend classes beside white students. In 1957, nine Black students were to begin classes at Little Rock Central High School, but Governor Orval Faubus attempted to block their attendance by calling in the National Guard. Additionally, more than 1,000 white protestors gathered at the school to voice their opposition to the federal desegregation law. Then-president Dwight D. Eisenhower called in federal troops to Little Rock. The troops escorted the Little Rock Nine into the school.

Best Time to Visit: This attraction is open daily between 9:00 a.m. and 4:30 p.m., year-round.

Pass/Permit/Fees: There is no fee to visit the Little Rock Central High School National Historic Site.

Closest City or Town: Little Rock

How to Get There: From I-630: Take Exit 2B for Dr. Martin Luther King Drive, and go south to W. Daisy L. Gatson Bates Drive. Turn right, and drive for 0.5 miles. You'll see the visitor center on the right at the corner of Park Street and W. Daisy L. Gatson Bates Drive.

GPS Coordinates: 34.7385° N, -92.2976° W

Did You Know? Guided tours of the high school are available but require advance reservations.

MacArthur Museum of Arkansas Military History

This museum's purpose is to showcase the state of Arkansas's military heritage from its beginnings as a territory to the present. It is located in the Tower Building of the Little Rock Arsenal. You'll discover artifacts that colorfully tell the story of Arkansas's role in various military actions both stateside and abroad. In addition to the permanent exhibits that are always available at the museum, you'll also be treated to temporary exhibits like *Undaunted Courage, Proven Loyalty: Japanese American Soldiers in World War II,* and *If These Walls Could Talk: The Little Rock Arsenal and the Old State House during the Civil War.*

Best Time to Visit: The museum is open between 10:00 a.m. and 5:00 p.m., Tuesday through Saturday, and from 1:00 p.m. to 5:00 p.m. on Sunday.

Pass/Permit/Fees: There is no fee to visit the MacArthur Museum of Arkansas Military History, but donations are welcome.

Closest City or Town: Little Rock

How to Get There: From I-630 East: Take Exit 1A onto E. 9th Street. Travel 0.6 miles to MacArthur Park, where the museum is located.

GPS Coordinates: 34.7391° N, -92.2653° W

Did You Know? The Arsenal Building was built in 1840 to protect Arkansas from Native American attacks.

Metro Streetcar

A 3.4-mile streetcar system known as the Metro Streetcar operates between Little Rock and North Little Rock. There are ten streetcar employees who operate three historic replica streetcars along the system, which serves more than 100,000 riders every year. This old-fashioned means of travel is a unique way to see the downtown areas of Little Rock and North Little Rock. You'll get to cross the Arkansas River, pass the Clinton Presidential Center, view Heifer International, and take your pick of a variety of restaurants, shops, bars, and cultural attractions at the Little Rock River Market and Creative Corridor. Electric streetcars have been in operation in the Little Rock area since 1891, but the replicas have only been around since 2004 when the attraction opened under the River Rail Streetcar name.

Best Time to Visit: The streetcars operate daily from about 8:30 a.m. to 10:00 p.m.

Pass/Permit/Fees: A one-way ride is $2.70 per person, and a round-trip ride is $5.40 per person.

Closest City or Town: Little Rock

How to Get There: From Fort Smith: Take I-40 East for 154 miles to E. 2nd Street in Little Rock. Take Exit 141A, then continue 0.2 miles to reach the station.

GPS Coordinates: 34.7602° N, -92.2670° W

Did You Know? The streetcars used on the Metro Streetcar route are similar to the Birney streetcars used in Little Rock until after World War II.

Museum Of Discovery

The Museum of Discovery, originally dubbed the Museum of Natural History & Antiquities, opened on Main Street in Little Rock in 1927. The museum moved to City Hall two years later. The museum's third location in MacArthur Park followed a seven-year closure starting in 1935 when the city determined it needed the space in City Hall for city business. Renamed the Museum of Discovery in 1998, the museum moved to its current location at River Market. It is now the premier technology and science center in Arkansas with the mission of igniting a passion for STEM domains through interactive experiences.

Best Time to Visit: The Museum of Discovery is open Wednesday through Saturday from 9:00 a.m. to 5:00 p.m. and on Sunday from 1:00 p.m. to 5:00 p.m. Since the museum is indoors, it is a great attraction to visit any time of the year.

Pass/Permit/Fees: Adult admission is $10.00. Children ages 12 and younger, seniors ages 60 and older, teachers, city employees, and military members are $8.00.

Closest City or Town: Little Rock

How to Get There: From Fort Smith: Take I-40 East for 154 miles to E. 2nd Street in Little Rock. Take Exit 141A, and follow the road for 0.1 miles to President Clinton Avenue, where the museum is located.

GPS Coordinates: 34.7485° N, -92.2647° W

Did You Know? The original museum featured, among other oddities, the head of a Chicago criminal.

Old State House Museum

The Old State House is the original capitol building for the state of Arkansas and has overseen some of the most notable events in the state's history. These include when the state was admitted to the Union in 1836, when the state seceded from the Union in 1861, and when native son, William Clinton, was elected President of the United States in 1992 and 1996. Built in 1833 in the Greek Revival style, the Old State House has been a museum since 1947, but it was supplanted by a new capitol building in 1915. Its current purpose is to preserve, share, and celebrate the history of the state and its people.

Best Time to Visit: The Old State House Museum is open Tuesday through Saturday from 9:00 a.m. to 5:00 p.m. and on Sunday from 1:00 p.m. to 5:00 p.m. The best time to visit is in the summer when it will be free from school tours.

Pass/Permit/Fees: There is no fee to visit the Old State House Museum, but donations are appreciated.

Closest City or Town: Little Rock

How to Get There: From Fort Smith: Take I-40 East for 154 miles to E. 2nd Street in Little Rock. Take Exit 141A, and travel for 0.4 miles to Ashley Street, where the museum is located.

GPS Coordinates: 34.7499° N, -92.2725° W

Did You Know? In a debate over taxes that took place in the Old State House in 1937, Speaker of the House John Wilson stabbed Representative Joseph J. Anthony to death.

Pinnacle Mountain

As the closest state park to Little Rock, Pinnacle Mountain is popular with locals and tourists alike. It offers more than 15 miles of hiking and biking trails, including 7 miles of rigorous mountain biking trails. It's a wonderful place to hold a reunion or party, as there are several covered pavilions and meeting rooms that can be rented. The mountain itself is 1,000 feet above sea level and is the convergence point of three rivers, making for gorgeous views and picturesque hikes.

Best Time to Visit: In April and May, the wildflowers will be in bloom throughout the park.

Pass/Permit/Fees: There is no fee to visit the park unless you reserve a pavilion, which is $85.00 per day. The visitor center meeting room is $75.00 per use, and the Scenic Overlook is $42.00 per hour.

Closest City or Town: Little Rock

How to Get There: From Little Rock: Take I-430 to Exit 9, which is about 1 mile south of the Arkansas River. Take Cantrell Road (Highway 10) west for about 2 miles to Pinnacle Valley Road. Follow the signs to the entrance.

GPS Coordinates: 34.8362° N, -92.4706° W

Did You Know? The Arkansas Arboretum is located at Pinnacle Mountain State Park. This 71-acre attraction exhibits the native flora that represents Arkansas's six natural divisions. Not only can you enjoy these exhibits, but there is also a 0.6-mile interpretive trail available to explore as well.

River Market District

The River Market District is the main downtown neighborhood of Little Rock. It features entertainment venues, restaurants, bars, art galleries, shops, museums, a library, and much more. It was developed by the City of Little Rock in conjunction with the Downtown Partnership to revitalize the downtown area and make it a cultural experience that features attractions for everyone of all ages. Be sure to stop by La Petite Roche Plaza and see the little rock for which Little Rock is named. French explorer Jean-Baptiste Bernard de la Harpe referred to this small rock outcrop as the "Little Rock" to differentiate it from the "Big Rock" further upriver.

Best Time to Visit: Events are always happening at the River Market District, but summer is the most popular time to visit because of the warm weather.

Pass/Permit/Fees: There is no fee to visit the River Market District unless you plan to attend an event that requires a paid ticket.

Closest City or Town: Little Rock

How to Get There: From Fort Smith: Take I-40 East for 154 miles to Arkansas Highway 10 West/S. Cumberland Street in Little Rock. Take Exit 141A, and drive for 0.2 miles to President Clinton Avenue.

GPS Coordinates: 34.7484° N, -92.2661° W

Did You Know? You can get a little taste of Korea by visiting the H.U. Lee International Gate and Garden located at 101 E. Markham Street in the River Market District.

Rock Town Distillery

This artisan craft distillery is the first legal distillery in the state of Arkansas since Prohibition. Only Arkansas grains from within a 125-mile radius from the distillery are used to create the spirits produced at Rock Town. The results have been nothing short of fantastic, as they have won several awards, including the 2015 U.S. Micro Whiskey of the Year award from Jim Murray's Whisky Bible. The distillery was founded by Phil Brandon in 2010, and since then, it has expanded its market to numerous U.S. states, the United Kingdom, and Canada.

Best Time to Visit: Tours are available daily at 2:00 p.m., 4:00 p.m., and 7:00 p.m., but they require advance online reservations. The tasting room is open from 11:00 a.m. to 9:00 p.m. every day except Monday, when the distillery is closed, and on Saturday, when it's open until 11:00 p.m.

Pass/Permit/Fees: Tours are $15 per person.

Closest City or Town: Little Rock

How to Get There: From Fort Smith: Take I-40 East for 155 miles to W. 11th Street in Little Rock. Take Exit 1B onto W. 11th Street. Follow the street to S. Louisiana Street, and travel for 0.2 miles to reach the distillery.

GPS Coordinates: 34.7380° N, -92.2722° W

Did You Know? Cocktail classes taught by some of the most talented bartenders in Arkansas are available at the distillery. They start at $30 per person and last for 1.5 hours.

The Arkansas River Trail System

This 88-mile loop takes hikers, bikers, skaters, and other outdoor activity lovers throughout Arkansas, passing through Little Rock, North Little Rock, Conway, and Maumelle. An offshoot loop of this trail extends 15.6 miles from the Clinton Presidential Bridge in Little Rock to the Big Dam Bridge and back. The trail system includes access to 38 parks, six museums, and more than 5,000 acres of local, state, and federal open land. You'll be amazed at the diversity of landscapes and habitats you'll pass at different points on the trail. The flat-terrain trail is accessible to people of all ages, abilities, and fitness levels.

Best Time to Visit: Spring and fall are the best times to visit the Arkansas River Trail System because the weather is cooler than in the summer but not too cold to enjoy the activities.

Pass/Permit/Fees: There is no fee to visit the Arkansas River Trail System.

Closest City or Town: Little Rock

How to Get There: From Fort Smith: Take I-40 East for 153 miles to Cypress Street in North Little Rock. Take Exit 141B, then follow the road for 0.8 miles to the trailhead.

GPS Coordinates: 34.9071° N, -92.4470° W

Did You Know? The two bridges that you'll cross while using the Arkansas River Trail System used to be railroad bridges. The Clinton Presidential Park Bridge was originally built in 1899 and was renamed in May 2010 after former president Bill Clinton, who hails from Arkansas.

William J. Clinton Presidential Library and Museum

Former president William "Bill" J. Clinton once called Little Rock his home, and as such, a library and museum were constructed in the city in his honor. The entire archive of documents from Clinton's presidency is housed at the library, but you'll also be able to enjoy a variety of other exhibits. The museum features replicas of the Cabinet Room and the Oval Office, the presidential limousine, a timeline of Clinton's presidency, and various displays about life in the White House.

Best Time to Visit: The library and museum are open Wednesday through Saturday from 10:00 a.m. to 4:00 p.m. and on Sunday from 1:00 p.m. to 5:00 p.m. As it is indoors, it is comfortable to visit any time of the year.

Pass/Permit/Fees: Adult admission is $10, while children between the ages of 6 and 17 are $6. Seniors ages 62 and older are $8. Children ages five and under and active-duty military are free.

Closest City or Town: Little Rock

How to Get There: From Fort Smith: Take I-40 East for 154 miles to E. 2nd Street in Little Rock. Take Exit 141A, and drive for 0.4 miles to President Clinton Avenue, where the museum is located.

GPS Coordinates: 34.7470° N, -92.2584° W

Did You Know? Be sure to check out the temporary exhibit that's on display during your visit.

Witt Stephens Jr. Central Arkansas Nature Center

Part of the River Market District in Little Rock, the Witt Stephens Jr. Central Arkansas Nature Center opened in 2008. It features a 16,232-square-foot building with exhibits that highlight the role of fish and wildlife management in the community. You'll learn about many projects that were managed by the Arkansas Game & Fish Commission throughout its history and discover the ways in which the commission protects Arkansas waters and the wilderness today. The location of the center along the Arkansas River provides visitors with the opportunity to watch various wildlife activities, which can be rare in an urban setting. Be sure to also visit the aquariums, theater, and gift shop at the center before you leave.

Best Time to Visit: The center is open Tuesday through Saturday from 8:30 a.m. to 4:30 p.m.

Pass/Permit/Fees: The nature center is free to visit.

Closest City or Town: Little Rock

How to Get There: From Fort Smith: Take I-40 East for 154 miles to E. 2nd Street in Little Rock. Take Exit 141A, then drive 0.4 miles to President Clinton Avenue to reach the center.

GPS Coordinates: 34.7488° N, -92.2641° W

Did You Know? In the theater, you'll see a 10-minute multimedia presentation that focuses on the Arkansas Game & Fish Commission.

Mammoth Spring

With more than 9 million gallons flowing each hour, Mammoth Spring is the largest spring in the country and one of the largest in the world. The park features a 10-acre lake that flows into the Spring River, one of the most famous water sources in the Ozarks. You can also explore an 1886 Frisco train depot, play ball on the baseball diamond, climb around on the playground, or enjoy lunch in the picnic area.

Best Time to Visit: The mild temperatures of spring and fall make these seasons the best time to visit this state park. The humidity will be lower, and you're more likely to see an abundance of waterfowl in the spring than during other times of the year.

Pass/Permit/Fees: Admission to the park is free, and it is open daily between 8:00 a.m. and dusk. There is a cost to rent canoes and kayaks to use on the lake.

Closest City or Town: Mammoth Spring

How to Get There: From Little Rock: Take I-630 East to US-167. Drive for 135 miles to Arkansas 289, then continue onto US-63. Turn left onto US-63, and you'll arrive at Mammoth Spring State Park.

GPS Coordinates: 36.4958° N, -91.5355° W

Did You Know? The U.S. Department of the Interior declared Mammoth Park a national natural landmark in 1972, 15 years after the state park was established in 1957.

Queen Wilhelmina State Park

This state park is located on top of Rich Mountain, the second-highest mountain in Arkansas. Originally, the park was the site of a Victorian resort called Wilhelmina Inn. Referred to as the "castle in the sky," the resort was popular for its breathtaking views and mild summer temperatures. Today, the park lodge is still the main attraction (other than the views), with 40 rooms and the Queen's Restaurant, which serves up delicious southern fare.

Best Time to Visit: For the clearest views from atop Rich Mountain, visit Queen Wilhelmina State Park in the winter.

Pass/Permit/Fees: There is no fee to visit Queen Wilhelmina State Park, but there is a charge to stay overnight at the lodge.

Closest City or Town: Mena

How to Get There: From Little Rock: Take I-30 West for 102 miles to Arkansas 88 West. Continue for 29.4 miles to US-59 North/US-71 North in Mena. Take US-59 North for 12.6 miles to Arkansas 272 West, then turn left to arrive at the park's entrance.

GPS Coordinates: 34.6856° N, -94.3704° W

Did You Know? The original resort was built to house passengers on the Kansas City, Pittsburg, and Gulf Railroad. Because the majority of the railroad's investors were Dutch, they named the resort after the Queen of the Netherlands.

Cedar Falls

Located in Petit Jean State Park, Cedar Falls is a 95-foot waterfall surrounded by cliffs and vertical walls. Visitors cannot swim in the pool under the falls, but they can get spectacular overhead views of Cedar Falls by taking a short hike to Cedar Falls Overlook. A wheelchair-accessible trail leads to a lookout deck that provides an unobstructed view of the falls. The hike to the bottom of Cedar Falls will bring you to a narrow bridge that crosses Cedar Creek. Along the way, you'll be treated to giant rock formations and picturesque tree stands that are perfect for selfies and group photos.

Best Time to Visit: Waterfall views are ideal during winter and spring.

Pass/Permit/Fees: There is no fee to visit Petit Jean State Park or to hike to Cedar Falls. If you stay the night, there is a daily camping fee. Cabins start at $106 per night.

Closest City or Town: Morrilton

How to Get There: From Little Rock: Take I-40 West to Exit 108 in Morrilton. Continue on Highway 9/113 South for 5 miles to Oppelo, then turn right onto Highway 154. Take Highway 154 to the park's entrance. The trail to Cedar Falls starts behind Mather Lodge.

GPS Coordinates: 35.1471° N, -92.9076° W

Did You Know? Cedar Falls is the second-most photographed place in Arkansas. Only Whitaker Point is more popular for photos.

Petit Jean State Park

Petit Jean State Park is the first state park in Arkansas. Its centerpiece is Petit Jean Mountain and scenic Cedar Falls. There are over 20 miles of hiking trails in the park, where you will pass by incredible geological formations and view ancient pictographs. Once you get to the peak of the mountain, you'll be 1,120 feet above the Arkansas River Valley and treated to awe-inspiring views of the gorgeous landscape. To visit Petit Jean's Gravesite, make your way to Stout's Point on the mountain's east side.

Best Time to Visit: October and November are the best months to visit Petit Jean State Park to see the incredible colors as the leaves change with the season.

Pass/Permit/Fees: It is free to visit Petit Jean State Park unless you're staying overnight. Rates vary for lodges, cabins, and camping, so it's best to contact the park directly.

Closest City or Town: Morrilton

How to Get There: From Little Rock: Take I-40 West to Exit 108 in Morrilton. Continue onto Highway 9/113 South for 5 miles to Oppelo, then turn right onto Highway 154. Take Highway 154 to the park's entrance.

GPS Coordinates: 35.1242° N, -92.9235° W

Did You Know? Petit Jean State Park got its name from a young 18th-century French girl who disguised herself as a boy so that she could secretly join a group of explorers to the New World. She is buried atop Petit Jean Mountain.

Lake Fort Smith State Park

At the western end of the 240-mile Ozark Highlands Trail, Lake Fort Smith State Park is popular with hikers, backpackers, and mountain bikers. However, fishing, kayaking, swimming, and camping are also available throughout the park. Note that while there is a 1,400-acre lake in the park, visitors cannot swim there. They must swim in the campground swimming pool only. There are 30 campsites for RVs, 10 cabins, a marina, group lodges, and a visitor center located on the property. A playground, splash pad, and wading pool are also available for guests.

Best Time to Visit: Spring and fall are the best seasons to visit the park, as its lower elevation keeps it hot in the summer.

Pass/Permit/Fees: There is no fee to visit Lake Fort Smith State Park, but there are fees to camp overnight.

Closest City or Town: Mountainburg

How to Get There: From Fort Smith: Take I-540 East for 25.1 miles to Arkansas Highway 282 East/US-71 in Crawford County. Take Exit 34 onto US-71 North, then travel 7 miles to the park's entrance.

GPS Coordinates: 35.6960° N, -94.1188° W

Did You Know? In the park's 8,000square-foot visitor center, you can see a replica covered wagon and pioneer log cabin, along with other exhibits that highlight the region's early history.

Blanchard Springs Caverns

There are four tours that visitors can take of the Blanchard Springs Caverns, including the Dripstone Trail, the Discovery Trail, the Discovery in the Dark Headlamp Tour, and the Wild Cave Tour. Each tour is led by Forest Service guides and takes guests through the caverns, where they'll see an underground river, the world's largest flowstone, and many other underground marvels. The Dripstone Trail is designed for people of all ages, and strollers are allowed. The Discovery Trail is more rigorous than the Dripstone Trail and includes 700 stairs to take you to the lower part of the caverns. For a more extensive tour, take the Wild Cave Tour to visit the undeveloped portions of the middle caverns.

Best Time to Visit: As with most caves, the Blanchard Springs Caverns stay at 58°F all year long, which makes it a pleasant attraction for any time of the year.

Pass/Permit/Fees: Adult admission for either the Dripstone Trail or the Discovery Trail is $14.00. Children between the ages of 6 and 15 are $9.00. The Wild Cave Tour is $85 per person, regardless of age.

Closest City or Town: Mountain View

How to Get There: From Mountain View: Take Arkansas 14 North for 15 miles to the entrance of the caverns.

GPS Coordinates: 35.9639° N, -92.1893° W

Did You Know? Blanchard Springs Caverns is a three-level cave system that includes the Living Cave, which is constantly growing and changing even today.

Mirror Lake

A 3-acre lake stocked full of rainbow trout; Mirror Lake is a haven for fishermen of all skill levels. Its waters are fed from the cool, 58°F Blanchard Spring Caverns, making the lake a clean, clear water source. While the lake itself is fairly small, it may just be the prettiest lake in the entire state. There is a two-tiered waterfall that flows over the stone dam, and the entire lake is surrounded by lush forest, which is reflected in the clear, calm waters that give the lake its name.

Best Time to Visit: The best time to visit Mirror Lake is in the spring when the fish are biting and the water is high, making the waterfall full and fast-flowing. The trees will also be in bloom, which makes this setting even more gorgeous than normal.

Pass/Permit/Fees: There is no fee to visit Mirror Lake.

Closest City or Town: Mountain View

How to Get There: From Mountain View: Take Arkansas Highway 14 North for 14 miles to the entrance.

GPS Coordinates: 35.9651° N, -92.1702° W

Did You Know? You can easily get to the nearby Blanchard Springs Caverns using a trail that takes you from the lake to the entrance of the caves. The hike is an easy 2 miles, making it perfect for families with young children. You will see the waterfall and the remnants of an old stone mill on your way to the caverns.

White Rock Mountain

If you're looking for a unique place to hold a large gathering, such as a reunion or retreat, you'll love the natural stone cabins on White Rock Mountain. Situated 2,260 feet above sea level, you and your guests will get a true mountain living experience. The lodge accommodates up to 30 people and is wheelchair accessible. The three cabins include stone fireplaces and rustic furniture. If you'd rather camp outside, there are eight camping sites with fire pits and tent pads.

Best Time to Visit: Fall is the best time to visit White Rock Mountain because of the incredible views of autumn foliage and the cooler temperatures.

Pass/Permit/Fees: There is a $3.00 day use fee per vehicle and additional rental costs for the cabins, lodge, and campsites. Campsites are $15 per night, cabins are $99 per night, and the lodge is $175 per night.

Closest City or Town: Mulberry

How to Get There: From Mulberry: Take Arkansas 215 North for 15 miles, then take Forest Service Road 1505 for 8 miles (part of this will be unpaved road). Turn west on Forest Service Road 1003, and follow for 2.5 miles to the lodge.

GPS Coordinates: 35.6923° N, -93.9561° W

Did You Know? White Rock Mountain gets its name from the lichen that grows on the bluffs and appears white from a distance.

The Crater of Diamonds

As mentioned in the overview of Arkansas, the state is home to the only place in the U.S. where visitors can look for real diamonds right where they developed. The 37-acre field is littered with minerals, gemstones, and, yes, diamonds. While you can bring your own manual mining equipment (no motors or batteries allowed), you can also rent tools directly from the park.

Best Time to Visit: The mine is open all year, but in the summer months, you'll want to visit as early as possible. Since the park opens at 8:00 a.m., you should be ready to go at that time to beat the heat. The fall and spring will allow you to mine comfortably at any time of the day.

Pass/Permit/Fees: Adults are $10.00 each, and children between the ages of 6 and 12 are $6.00. If you buy tickets online, you'll also pay a fee of $1.50 for adults and $1.30 for children

Closest City or Town: Murfreesboro

How to Get There: From Little Rock: Take I-30 West to Exit 73 for Arkadelphia. Take Arkansas 51 West and Arkansas 26 to Murfreesboro. At the courthouse square, take Arkansas 301 southeast for 2 miles to reach the park entrance.

GPS Coordinates: 34.0325° N, -93.6729° W

Did You Know? Visitors have found more than 33,100 diamonds at the Crater of Diamonds since 1972, including the 40.23-carat Uncle Sam diamond, the largest to ever be discovered in the United States.

Natural Dam

Located in the Boston Mountain range, Natural Dam offers an easily accessed waterfall and incredible views of the Ozark Mountains. The falls are about eight feet high and 200 feet wide, and you're able to see it from your car if you don't want to stop. However, it's one of the most picturesque places to enjoy a picnic without requiring a hike first. The Natural Dam spans the entire Mountain Fork Creek, which makes it an incredible sight to see! While the dam looks man-made, it was formed entirely by natural forces and represented a unique geological wonder.

Best Time to Visit: The falls flow best right after rain, so spring is the best time to visit. In the summer, you may not see much activity at the falls, especially if there hasn't been a lot of rain.

Pass/Permit/Fees: This attraction is free.

Closest City or Town: Natural Dam

How to Get There: From I-40 at Van Buren, take Arkansas Highway 59 North. You'll cross a bridge before you enter the town of Natural Dam. When you see the sign for Natural Dam Falls, turn left, and you'll see the falls from the road.

GPS Coordinates: 35.6487° N, -94.3947° W

Did You Know? Natural Dam Falls is known as "Little Niagara" due to its resemblance to Niagara Falls on a much smaller scale.

Big Dam Bridge

The Big Dam Bridge is the longest bicycle and pedestrian bridge in North America. Towering 90 feet above the Arkansas River, the bridge got its name because of its length of 4,226 feet and its location atop the Murray Lock and Dam. The bridge connects more than 14 miles of trails that pass through Little Rock and North Little Rock. It allows foot travelers and cyclists to access 70,000 acres of park land throughout the area. The bridge was originally named the Murray Bridge but became known as the Big Dam Bridge by Pulaski County Judge F.G. Villines, who, during an impassioned speech about financing the project, said, "We're going to build that dam bridge." The bridge, which cost $12.8 million, opened to public foot and bicycle traffic in September 2006.

Best Time to Visit: The bridge is open all year.

Pass/Permit/Fees: There is no fee to visit the Big Dam Bridge.

Closest City or Town: North Little Rock

How to Get There:
From Fort Smith: Take I-40 East for 147 miles to Arkansas State Highway 100 East/Crystal Hill Road in North Little Rock. Take Exit 12, then travel 1.5 miles on Cook's Landing Road to the bridge.

GPS Coordinates: 34.7934° N, -92.3586° W

Did You Know? Several races take place across the Big Dam Bridge, including the Big Dam Bridge 100 Cycling Tour, the BDB Twilight 5k race, and the BDB Duathlon.

Mulberry River

If you're looking for a river to raft, the Mulberry River will give you a wild ride, especially during the spring, when the waters run fast and heavy. It has a class II/III rating for its rapids and receives praise as a fun and exciting rafting river. In the summer, when the river calms down, you'll find places along it that are perfect for swimming and wading. You can't beat the Ozark Mountain surroundings as you play or relax in the water. Fishermen also find the river full of smallmouth, largemouth, and spotted bass, especially in late spring and early summer.

Best Time to Visit: Spring offers the best rapids for rafting and an abundance of bass for fishing.

Pass/Permit/Fees: There is no fee to visit the Mulberry River, but a fishing license is required if you decide to drop a line.

Closest City or Town: Ozark

How to Get There: From Ozark: Take W. Commercial Street west for 1 mile toward S. 4th Street. Turn right onto Arkansas Highway 23 North/N. 18th Street, then take Arkansas 23 North for 17.1 miles to Arkansas Highway 215 East. Continue for 5.8 miles to the Mulberry River.

GPS Coordinates: 35.4667° N, -94.0418° W

Did You Know? The Mulberry River is 70 miles long and a tributary of the Arkansas River. Most of the river runs through the Ozark National Forest.

Crowley's Ridge

Located in northeast Arkansas, Crowley's Ridge is a state park that features a 31-acre lake for fishing and a 3.5-acre lake for swimming. Boat rentals are also available at the marina, and camping is allowed in one of the 26 campsites in the park. Five bunk cabins on the property are ideal for group outings. Families may also enjoy the four cabins that feature kitchens and fireplaces for a rustic getaway. The park used to be a Native American campground before becoming a homestead for settlers in the 1800s. Crowley's Ridge is one of Arkansas's six original state parks.

Best Time to Visit: The park is well shaded, so a summer visit isn't out of the question, but fall and spring are the preferred seasons to visit Crowley's Ridge.

Pass/Permit/Fees: The park is free to visit unless you are staying overnight.

Closest City or Town: Paragould

How to Get There: From Paragould: Take US-412 West for 9 miles, then turn south on Highway 168. Travel for 2 miles to reach the park's entrance.

GPS Coordinates: 36.0434° N, -90.6640° W

Did You Know? Crowley's Ridge is named after Benjamin F. Crowley, who was a soldier in the War of 1812. His land grant became the first pioneer settlement in northeast Arkansas.

Mount Magazine State Park

Located in the Ozark and St. Francis national forests, Mount Magazine State Park offers incredible views atop Arkansas's highest point of 2,753 feet. Just about any outdoor activity, you can imagine is available in this park, including hiking, mountain biking, horseback riding, ATV riding, rock climbing, camping, and more. At the lodge, you'll have access to a heated indoor swimming pool, game room, and fitness center. It's an ideal location for large events, including business conferences, reunions, and weddings.

Best Time to Visit: This is one park that has benefits no matter what time of year you visit. In the winter, you can enjoy the fireplace pit, hot tubs, and heated pool. In autumn, you'll see the amazing fall foliage as it changes colors. It's even comfortable in summer because the altitude keeps the temperatures cool.

Pass/Permit/Fees: There is no fee to visit the park, but rates vary for overnight stays at the lodge, cabins, and campsites.

Closest City or Town: Paris

How to Get There: From Paris: Take Highway 309 South for 16 miles to reach the park's entrance.

GPS Coordinates: 35.1687° N, -93.6261° W

Did You Know? The original lodge was part of a resort town that drew visitors to the park because of the cooler summer temperatures. It burned in 1971 and was rebuilt in 1998.

Magnolia Falls

Magnolia Falls is a 26-foot waterfall located in the Buffalo River area in southwest Newton County. The road to the falls is not marked, but you should be able to spot the gravel road that will lead you there. The trailhead is an old Jeep trail that winds through the forest and deposits you directly next to the waterfall. It's not an easy hike, but it is very scenic, so you'll want to go slow anyway to take in the views. You are likely to be the only visitors on the day you go because this waterfall is not a prominent attraction, but you will be glad you took the time to see it.

Best Time to Visit: For the best weather, visit Magnolia Falls between March and May.

Pass/Permit/Fees: There is no fee to visit Magnolia Falls.

Closest City or Town: Pettigrew

How to Get There: Take Arkansas Highway 21 for 2.5 miles south of Mossville Church. Turn west on County Road 6/Forest Road 1462. Travel about 0.3 miles to a pull-off area for parking. You will see a sign that says "Wilderness Access" to your left. This is the entrance to the trailhead.

GPS Coordinates: 35.8628° N, -93.3984° W

Did You Know? There are actually four waterfalls in this area, including Magnolia Falls, Woods Boys Falls, Stahle Falls, and Hadlock Cascade. They are all within walking distance of each other, and even though Magnolia Falls is the most picturesque, the others are worth seeing as well.

Bowers Hollow Falls

This 56-foot-tall waterfall is one of the most spectacular sights in the Ozarks. The falls are located in the Upper Buffalo Wilderness area of the Ozark National Forest. You will find the path to the falls well-traveled and easy to follow. The most challenging section is the last few feet to the top of the falls, which are steep and covered with vegetation. You can also get to the bottom of the falls by crossing the creek above the waterfall and following the bluff line until you see a break that allows you to climb down. It will be very slick, so take care if you attempt this descent. The pool at the bottom is worth the effort, though.

Best Time to Visit: In the spring, the creek will be running high, making the waterfalls full and fast flowing.

Pass/Permit/Fees: There is no fee to visit Bowers Hollow Falls.

Closest City or Town: Ponca

How to Get There: From Ponca: Take Arkansas Highway 43 South to Arkansas Highway 21. Turn left and continue for 1.2 miles. You will cross two bridges before turning right onto Cave Mountain Road. Travel up this gravel road for 8.6 miles until you reach FR 1410-B. If you do not have a four-wheel-drive car, park here and walk to the trailhead.

GPS Coordinates: 35.8544° N, -93.4577° W

Did You Know? You are able to swim in the pool at the base of the waterfall, but be aware that the water is very cold!

Centerpoint Trail to Goat Trail

While the Centerpoint Trail to Goat Trail route is one of the most heavily used, it's also one of the most difficult. Located in the Buffalo National River, the total trail is 5.9 miles long and features a downhill hike to the Big Bluff that overlooks the Buffalo River. This hike is not recommended for small children or for anyone who is afraid of heights. However, once you get to the top, the views from the Goat Trail outcrop are amazing. Be aware that the hike out is all uphill, which is part of what makes this hike so challenging. The path is well traveled and clearly marked.

Best Time to Visit: In early spring, the trail tends to be muddy, so late spring and early fall are the best times to explore the trail. Photographers will want to visit in the afternoon to get the best lighting.

Pass/Permit/Fees: There is no fee to travel this route.

Closest City or Town: Ponca

How to Get There: From Boxley: Take Arkansas Highway 43 to Ponca. About 3.5 miles outside of Ponca, you will find the trailhead to the Centerpoint Trail to Goat Trail route.

GPS Coordinates: 36.0524° N, -93.3231° W

Did You Know? The Goat Trail gets its name from domesticated goats that were either let loose in the forest or escaped captivity from the original pioneers in the area. They eventually turned wild, and some descendants can still be seen today in the upper Buffalo River wilderness.

Hawksbill Crag

Also known as Whitaker Point, Hawksbill Crag is the most photographed formation in Arkansas. The crag juts out over a vast valley, which makes it look treacherous, and it can be if you're not careful. Once you reach the crag, you'll get spectacular views of the forested valley below, but if you travel with a friend, you'll also get an amazing shot of you standing on this precarious outcrop. The hike to the crag is moderately challenging, and it's about 2 miles from the trailhead.

Best Time to Visit: To see one of the most spectacular sunrises you'll ever witness, hike to Hawksbill Crag in the early morning before the sun comes up. If you plan to go in the morning, summer is the best time for this hike. Otherwise, it's the coolest in the spring and fall.

Pass/Permit/Fees: There is no fee to hike to Hawksbill Crag.

Closest City or Town: Ponca

How to Get There: From Harrison: Take Highway 43 South to Highway 21. Continue through Boxley Valley. Turn right on County Road 5/Cave Mountain Road, and go about 6 miles, where you'll see a sign for the trailhead to Hawksbill Crag.

GPS Coordinates: 35.8909° N, -93.4404° W

Did You Know? On the hike to Hawksbill Crag, you can see three different waterfalls: Mule Trails Falls, Thousand Kisses Falls and Haley Falls. You'll have to venture off the trail a bit and follow the signs to each waterfall.

Roark Bluff

If you're a photographer, you simply must visit Roark Bluff, as it is a masterpiece of nature. The sunrise is spectacular when it catches the bluff in the mornings, and the waterfalls are naturally gorgeous backdrops at any time of the day. Additionally, you can take a fairly easy hike to the top of the bluff and get an awe-inspiring view of the Steel Creek area below. This is not a busy trail, so you're almost sure to have the view to yourself. It's 2.2 miles round trip, and it's a wonderful place to have a picnic as long as you stay away from the ledge.

Best Time to Visit: Fall is the best time to visit Roark Bluff so that you can see the glorious fall colors of the changing leaves.

Pass/Permit/Fees: There is no fee to visit Roark Bluff.

Closest City or Town: Ponca

How to Get There: From Little Rock: Take I-40 West for 94.2 miles to US-64 West/E. Main Street in Lamar. Take Exit 64 onto Arkansas 21. Go north 60.3 miles to Roark Bluff.

GPS Coordinates: 36.0440° N, -93.3421° W

Did You Know? There are two amazing waterfalls in the Roark Bluff area: Roark Bluff Falls and V-Notch Falls. You can get to these waterfalls through Steel Creek Campground near Buffalo National River. Both can be seen from the road, so no hiking is necessary!

Beaver Lake

With 28,000 acres of clear water, there are plenty of activities available at Beaver Lake, including fishing, boating, water skiing, kayaking, swimming, wakeboarding, and scuba diving. Off the lake, there are dozens of hiking trails and areas for picnicking. Birdwatchers and wildlife lovers can also enjoy the abundance of animals in the park. They can often be seen from the well-maintained trails. The lake is full of bass and serves as a popular location for local and national fishing tournaments.

Best Time to Visit: Since water activities are the most popular thing to do at the lake, summer is the best time to visit.

Pass/Permit/Fees: There is a day-use fee of $4 per vehicle to access all developed recreation areas on Beaver Lake.

Closest City or Town: Rogers

How to Get There: From Fayetteville: Take US-71 North for 22 miles, then turn east on US-62 to reach the park's entrance.

GPS Coordinates: 36.3489° N, -93.9325° W

Did You Know? Beaver Lake was created when Beaver Lake Dam was completed in 1966. Dam construction cost $46.2 million, and it contains 748,000 cubic feet of concrete. It is the first of several dams in the area that are designed to control flooding in northwest Arkansas. The lake contains 1,952,000 acre-feet of water.

War Eagle Cavern

Located on Beaver Lake, War Eagle Cavern is the only lakeside cave entrance in the state. It is one of the easier cave tours as well, with only a few step-ups the entire way. You'll be treated to spectacular domes and other cave formations along the path, and you might even see some bats and salamanders as well. You can also bring strollers and dogs, which is very unusual for show caves. This makes it a great activity for all members of the family, even if you decide to go on a spur-of-the-moment visit when you're visiting the lake.

Best Time to Visit: The cave stays at a cool 58°F all year long, so it's a great activity in the summer, spring, and fall. The cavern is closed during December, January, and February.

Pass/Permit/Fees: Adult admission to the cave tour is $19.00, and children between the ages of 4 and 12 are $11.50.

Closest City or Town: Rogers

How to Get There: From Rogers: Go east on Walnut Street to the 8th Street intersection, then keep going straight (avoid turning onto this entrance to Highway 12). Look for signs, and turn east on Highway 12, then travel 15 miles to reach the cavern's entrance.

GPS Coordinates: 36.2953° N, -93.9045° W

Did You Know? If you're visiting Beaver Lake, you can take a boat to War Eagle Cavern. The cavern's boat dock is in Devils Gap Inlet.

Lake Dardanelle State Park

Lake Dardanelle State Park, which surrounds the 34,300-acre lake, is one of the largest state parks in Arkansas. It features a fishing pier, hiking trail, boardwalk, series of aquariums, visitor center, and meeting area. There are also 75 campsites in two distinct areas of the park, encompassing 16 Class AAA, 14 Class AA, and 45 Class B sites. Famous for its abundant fishing opportunities, Lake Dardanelle State Park is the site of major bass fishing tournaments. Both kayaks and bicycles can be rented in the park, depending on whether you want a water or land adventure.

Best Time to Visit: Bass fishing is best between April and May, but the lake will be quite crowded then. Fall is less crowded, but the fishing is not as good.

Pass/Permit/Fees: There is no fee to visit Lake Dardanelle State Park unless you stay overnight.

Closest City or Town: Russellville

How to Get There: From Russellville: Take Arkansas Highway 7 South to Arkansas Highway 326. Turn right on Arkansas Highway 326, and travel 4 miles to the park's entrance.

GPS Coordinates: 35.2830° N, -93.2030° W

Did You Know? Lake Dardanelle State Park is certified by the National Park Service as a site on the Trail of Tears water route. The Trail of Tears was the route Native Americans took as they were forcibly relocated in the 1830s.

Arvest Ballpark

This stadium is the home of the Northwest Arkansas Naturals, a minor league baseball team that is a member of the Double-A Central league. The stadium holds 7,305 fans and earned the title of Ballpark of the Year by baseballparks.com in 2008, its opening year. The main goal behind building the stadium was to bring a minor league team to Springdale, as then-mayor Jerre M. Van Hoose knew that a new stadium is a major draw for Major League Baseball-affiliated ballclubs. The local voters approved the construction of the new stadium in 2006 by a narrow margin. The stadium was designed by Populous, an architecture company in Kansas City, Missouri, and was built by Crossland Construction.

Best Time to Visit: The best time to visit Arvest Ballpark is during baseball season, which occurs in the spring, summer, and early fall.

Pass/Permit/Fees: The cost to visit Arvest Ballpark varies based on game and seat selection.

Closest City or Town: Springdale

How to Get There: From Little Rock: Take I-40 West for 198 miles to Don Tyson Parkway in Springdale. Take Exit 70, and continue on Don Tyson Parkway for 0.8 miles to the ballpark.

GPS Coordinates: 36.1605° N, -94.1946° W

Did You Know? The first baseball game played at Arvest Ballpark was between the home team Naturals and the San Antonio Missions on April 10, 2008.

Fly ARH (Arkansas Helicopters)

Are you looking to view Arkansas from a brand-new perspective? Try a helicopter from Fly ARH, the premier aviation company in northwest Arkansas. Fly over uptown Fayetteville, downtown Fayetteville, Beaver Lake, Crystal Bridges, and Eureka Springs. You can tour the entire area in a Robinson R44 helicopter. You'll never get a better view of the Ozarks than from overhead. If being a passenger for this experience just isn't daring enough, you can also take lessons to fly the helicopter yourself! Look for special flights like those offered on Valentine's Day or during the holidays for a one-of-a-kind experience.

Best Time to Visit: The helicopter can be reserved at any time of the year but will only fly during good weather. As such, summer is the best time to visit.

Pass/Permit/Fees: Tour prices begin at $75 per person for adults and $65 per person for children under the age of 13. The most expensive tour is the Ultimate Experience, which is $375 per adult and $365 per child.

Closest City or Town: Springdale

How to Get There: From Little Rock: Take I-40 West for 194 miles to US-71 North in Fayetteville. Travel 5 miles to reach Springdale Airport.

GPS Coordinates: 36.1749° N, -94.1223° W

Did You Know? If you're planning to visit Branson, Missouri, while you're in the Ozarks, consider taking the Branson Adventure Day flight from Fly ARH, which flies you directly to the famous Branson entertainment district.

Parsons Stadium

Parsons Stadium is a multipurpose facility that features the Rodeo of the Ozarks every June. Various events are held here each year, including professional bull-riding events, a demolition derby, a fall carnival, and a Christmas parade. Children can also attend the horse camp at the Rodeo of the Ozarks to learn about horses and the sport of rodeo in an effort to bring the lessons of a rich western heritage to a new generation. Camp attendees spend a full day participating in horse- and rodeo-related activities like crafts, roping, barrel racing, and riding. The Rodeo of the Ozarks first debuted in 1944 and attracted visitors from all over the country.

Best Time to Visit: If you want to see the rodeo, June is the best time to visit.

Pass/Permit/Fees: The fee to visit Parsons Stadium depends on the event and where your seats are located.

Closest City or Town: Springdale

How to Get There: From the north or south: Take I-49 to Exit 73 in Springdale. Turn east on Elm Springs Road. Follow this road, which will turn into Huntsville Road, to the light at Highway 265/Old Missouri Road. Turn right on Highway 265, and the stadium is located at the next stoplight.

GPS Coordinates: 36.1840° N, -94.1157° W

Did You Know? At the first rodeo in 1945, the bleachers on the north side of the stadium collapsed, sending 300 people to the hospital.

Sassafras Springs Vineyard & Winery

The 60-acre Sassafras Springs Vineyard & Winery opened in 2014, the fulfilled dream of Cheryl and Gene Long. Originally, the vineyard spanned just 15 acres, but with 3,000 visitors flocking to the winery each year, expansion became necessary soon after it opened. The venue is now one of the top locations for events in northwest Arkansas, and because it's a family operation, you're sure to notice special touches that large corporate ventures just don't have. This is due to the Longs' continued passion for discovering inventive ways to enhance their visitors' experiences, whether you're there for a wedding or just to sample their award-winning wines.

Best Time to Visit: Sassafras Springs Vineyard & Winery is open 11:00 a.m. to 7:00 p.m., Tuesday and Wednesday, and from 11:00 a.m. to 9:30 p.m., Thursday through Saturday.

Pass/Permit/Fees: A wine tasting is $10 for four 2-ounce pours and a keepsake wineglass stamped with the Sassafras logo. Rental rates vary.

Closest City or Town: Springdale

How to Get There: From Fort Smith: Take I-49 North for 59.3 miles to US-71 North in Fayetteville. Take the US-71 North exit, and follow E. Joyce Boulevard for 5.7 miles to E. Guy Terry Road, where the vineyard is located.

GPS Coordinates: 36.1283° N, -94.0666° W

Did You Know? The winery produces between 800 and 1,000 cases of wine each year.

Shiloh Museum of Ozark History

When the City of Springdale purchased a large collection of Native American artifacts in 1965 from long-time resident Guy Howard, city officials needed a place to store their acquisition. At first, they made use of a vacant building to identify, classify, and catalog the objects under the guidance of the University of Arkansas Museum staff, but soon, they organized a group to create a museum. In 1968, the museum opened to the public in the former Springdale Public Library building. After expanding to include the property next door to the library and adding four historical buildings to the lot, the museum moved into a new 22,000square-foot structure in 1991.

Best Time to Visit: The museum is open Monday through Friday from 10:00 a.m. to 5:00 p.m.

Pass/Permit/Fees: There is no fee to visit the Shiloh Museum of Ozark History.

Closest City or Town: Springdale

How to Get There: From I-49: Take Exit 73, then turn east on Elm Springs Road. This will turn into Huntsville Road. Drive for approximately 2 miles to Main Street. Turn right on Main Street, and the museum will be three blocks down on your left.

GPS Coordinates: 36.1874° N, -94.1320° W

Did You Know? The founders named the museum The Shiloh Museum after the settlement that was established in the 1940s. It was renamed the Shiloh Museum of Ozark History in 1993 to better reflect its purpose.

The Jones Center

The Jones Center is a 220,000square-foot facility for recreation, events, and education. It features an ice-skating arena, a junior Olympic-size lap swimming pool, an activity pool with a water slide, a bike park, basketball court, indoor track, fitness center, chapel, auditorium, and conference center. It is the training facility for several regional youth teams, including the NWA Hockey Association and the Aquahawgs swim team. Families can also access affordable activities for their children at the center, including gymnastics, aikido, figure skating, ballet, and taekwondo.

Best Time to Visit: The Jones Center is open Monday through Friday from 6:30 a.m. to 9:00 p.m. and from 7:30 a.m. to 9:00 p.m. on Saturday and Sunday. The fitness center opens and closes an hour earlier. Since it is indoors, you can visit any time of the year.

Pass/Permit/Fees: The cost to visit The Jones Center varies by activity.

Closest City or Town: Springdale

How to Get There: From the north or south: Take I-49 to Exit 73 for Elm Springs. Turn right from the south or left from the north. Follow this road as it crosses Thompson and turns into Huntsville Road. The facility is 1.1 miles from the Huntsville/US-71 intersection on the right.

GPS Coordinates: 36.1868° N, -94.1187° W

Did You Know? Membership rates are available, but drop-in participants are also welcome.

Tontitown Winery

Built in 1917, the "Taldo House" is the current home of Tontitown Winery and the former home of the "Dixie Pride Bonded Winery #40." Wine has been made here since 1923 by the family that is in charge of the process today. Nazzareno Ranalli started the tradition of making wine, and that tradition lives on through on-site wine production from grapes grown locally in Tontitown. Be sure to stop by the History Room to learn about the wine-making Italians who founded Tontitown and helped put it on the map for wine and grapes.

Best Time to Visit: The Tontitown Winery is open Monday through Thursday from 11:00 a.m. to 7:00 p.m., Friday and Saturday from 11:00 a.m. to 10:00 p.m., and Sunday from 12:00 p.m. to 5:00 p.m.

Pass/Permit/Fees: There is no fee to visit the Tontitown Winery, but there is a cost if you want to try the wine or get something to eat.

Closest City or Town: Springdale

How to Get There: From Little Rock: Take I-40 West for 197 miles to W. Sunset Avenue in Springdale. Take Exit 72 onto Sunset Avenue, and travel for 3.1 miles to reach the winery.

GPS Coordinates: 36.1806° N, -94.2350° W

Did You Know? The Tontitown Winery also hosts various events every week, including Wednesday Night BINGO, Sip & Sing, Beer & Hymns, and more. Check the website to find the dates of upcoming events.

Quigley's Castle

Billed as the "Ozarks' Strangest Dwelling," Quigley's Castle was the dream home of Elise Fioravanti Quigley, who lived from 1910 to 1984. Her husband, Albert Quigley, was bound and determined to give her the house of her dreams, which required abundant space for a growing family. Mrs. Quigley's design included 28 large windows, which couldn't be finished until three years after construction started because of the unavailability of glass during World War II. Other interesting features of the house include a section of bare earth inside the house to bring nature indoors, a rock wall that encompassed stones that Mrs. Quigley had been collecting since childhood, and the "butterfly" wall that displays her extensive butterfly collection.

Best Time to Visit: The museum is open from April through October from 10:00 a.m. and 4:30 p.m.

Pass/Permit/Fees: Adult admission is $7 per person, and children ages 14 and under are free.

Closest City or Town: Springs

How to Get There: From Fort Smith: Take I-49 North for 59.3 miles to US-71 North in Fayetteville. Take the US-71B Exit onto US-412 East, and drive for 38.9 miles to reach Quigley Castle Road in Carroll County.

GPS Coordinates: 36.3469° N, -93.7558° W

Did You Know? The Quigley Castle was once featured on HGTV and PBS's *Rare Visions and Roadside Revelations*.

Cane Creek Lake Trail

This 15.5-mile trail is located in Cane Creek State Park and will take you through a thick forest filled with dogwood trees. You'll cross three suspension bridges along the path, and the rolling hills are perfect for mountain bikers. This hike will take most of the day for cyclists and hikers alike, although it's not a particularly difficult route. Camping is available at the Cane Creek Lake Trail camping shelters, but you must acquire a permit from the visitor center. Expect to see a lot of wildlife on your way through the park, including beavers and eagles.

Best Time to Visit: Fall is the best time to hike or bike the Cane Creek Lake Trail. However, you will see water lilies blooming on the lake if you go in the summer.

Pass/Permit/Fees: There is no fee to visit the Cane Creek Lake Trail, but you do need a permit to camp overnight.

Closest City or Town: Star City

How to Get There: From Little Rock: Take I-530 South for 47.7 miles to Arkansas Highway 530. Take Exit 44, then follow Arkansas 530, Arkansas 212 East, and State Highway 293 for 25.7 miles to Grasshopper Circle. Take Grasshopper Circle to the park's entrance.

GPS Coordinates: 33.9306° N, -91.7710° W

Did You Know? You will cross more than 50 bridges if you hike or bike the entire length of the Cane Creek Lake Trail.

Devil's Den State Park

Located in northwest Arkansas, Devil's Den State Park encompasses nearly every type of natural wonder in the state. You can find caves, waterfalls, forests, bluffs, hiking trails, gorgeous sunrises and sunsets, and much more. A rock dam crosses Lee Creek to form the 8-acre Lake Devil, where fishing and boating are popular activities. Horseback riding, mountain biking, and backpacking are other reasons that visitors and locals love this iconic state park.

Best Time to Visit: Summer and fall are the best seasons to visit Devil's Den State Park because the fishing and other water activities can cool you down. In the fall, you'll see the splendor of the changing leaves and enjoy cooler temperatures.

Pass/Permit/Fees: There is no fee to visit Devil's Den State Park unless you stay the night. Cabin rentals are $190 per night, but campgrounds are cheaper.

Closest City or Town: West Fork

How to Get There: From Little Rock: Take I-40 West and I-49 North to Arkansas 74 West in Washington County. At Exit 45, turn left onto Arkansas 74 West, then travel 5.3 miles to reach the park's entrance.

GPS Coordinates: 35.7843° N, -94.2452° W

Did You Know? Archaeologists have found six prehistoric sites in Devil's Den State Park that indicate Native American tribes used the area as hunting grounds. The park gets its name from the nearly 60 crevice caves that legends say were hideouts for outlaws in the 1800s.

Lee Creek Valley

Located in Devil's Den State Park, Lee Creek Valley is a loop trail that provides 1 ¼ miles of moderately challenging hiking. Expect to find numerous fossils along the way, along with a seam of coal. The hike takes approximately one hour to complete the loop. There are also 30 miles of ATV trails available adjacent to the state park, which is also used by horseback riders, bicyclists, and hikers.

Best Time to Visit: Autumn is the best time to visit Lee Creek Valley, though it should be avoided entirely in the spring when the rains can flood the creek bed. Devil's Den State Park is an excellent place to visit all year round.

Pass/Permit/Fees: Lee Creek Valley is free to visit.

Closest City or Town: West Fork

How to Get There: Take I-540 South from Fayetteville for 8 miles to Exit 53 for West Fork. Take Arkansas 170 for 17 miles to Arkansas 220. Turn right on 220, which will turn into a dirt road. There are several trailheads available on 220.

GPS Coordinates: 35.6814° N, -94.3493° W

Did You Know? A rock dam in Devil's Den State Park spans Lee Creek to form Lake Devil.

Cossatot River State Park

Extending for 12 miles along the Cossatot River, this state park is a popular challenge for experienced kayakers and rafters who want to take on Class IV rapids. There are also four hiking trails that span almost 20 miles for visitors who aren't into riding the rapids. Of all the state parks in Arkansas, this is one of the most rustic, with only tent campsites available. There are no RV hookups and no water or electricity in the park. There are restrooms, fire pits, and grills that you can use while camping near the river.

Best Time to Visit: If you're a rafter or kayaker, the best time to visit Cossatot River State Park is in the spring when the runoff is high, and the water is fast. Otherwise, choose fall when the colors of the changing leaves are vivid.

Pass/Permit/Fees: There is no fee to visit Cossatot River State Park, but there is a $15 fee per night to camp in a tent space. The River Ridge Group Camp (also for tents only) is $79 per night.

Closest City or Town: Wickes

How to Get There: From Wickes: Take Pine Street South to S. 1st Street. Turn left on S. 1st Street, and drive to US-278 East/Baker Springs Road. Turn right on US-278/Baker Springs Road to arrive at the park's entrance.

GPS Coordinates: 34.4261° N, -94.3224° W

Did You Know? Cossatot River State Park is Arkansas's newest state park. The name Cossatot means "skull crusher," which comes from the wild rapids in the area.

Proper Planning

With this guide, you are well on your way to properly planning a marvelous adventure. When you plan your travels, you should become familiar with the area, save any maps to your phone for access without internet, and bring plenty of water—especially during the summer months. Depending on the adventure you choose, you will also want to bring snacks and even a lunch. For younger children, you should do your research and find destinations that best suit the needs of your family. Additionally, you should plan when to get gas, scout local lodgings, and figure out where to get food after you're finished. We've done our best to group these destinations based on nearby towns and cities to help make planning easier.

Dangerous Wildlife

There are several dangerous animals and insects you may encounter while hiking. With a good dose of caution and awareness, you can explore safely. Here is what you can do to keep yourself and your loved ones safe from dangerous flora and fauna while exploring:

- Keep to the established trails.
- Do not look under rocks, leaves, or sticks.
- Keep hands and feet out of small crawl spaces, bushes, covered areas, or crevices.
- Wear long sleeves and pants to keep arms and legs protected.
- Keep your distance should you encounter any dangerous wildlife or plants.

Limited Cell Service

Do not rely on cell service for navigation or emergencies. Always have a map with you, and let someone know where you are and for how long you intend to be gone, just in case.

First Aid Information

Always travel with a first aid kit in case of emergencies. Here are items that you should be certain to include in your primary first aid kit:

- Nitrile gloves
- Blister care products
- Waterproof bandages in multiple sizes
- Ace wrap and athletic tape
- Alcohol wipes and antibiotic ointment
- Irrigation syringe
- Tweezers, nail clippers, trauma shears, safety pins
- Small Ziplock bags for holding contaminated trash

It's a good practice to also keep a secondary first aid kit, especially when hiking, for more serious injuries or medical emergencies. Items in this should include:

- Blood clotting sponges
- Sterile gauze pads
- Trauma pads
- Moist burn pads
- Triangular bandages/sling
- Butterfly strips
- Tincture of benzoin
- Medications (ibuprofen, acetaminophen, antihistamine, aspirin, etc.)
- Thermometer
- CPR mask
- Wilderness medicine handbook
- Antivenom

There is so much more to explore, but this is a great start.

For information on all national parks, visit: www.nps.gov.

This site will give you information on up-to-date entrance fees and how to purchase a park pass for unlimited access to national and state parks. These sites will also introduce you to all of the trails of each park.

Always check before you travel to destinations to make sure that there are no closures. Some hikes close when there is heavy rain or snow in the area, and other parks close parts of their land to allow wildlife to migrate. Attractions may change their hours or temporarily shut down for various reasons. Check websites for the most up-to-date information.

Made in the USA
Las Vegas, NV
27 October 2022

58103124R00075